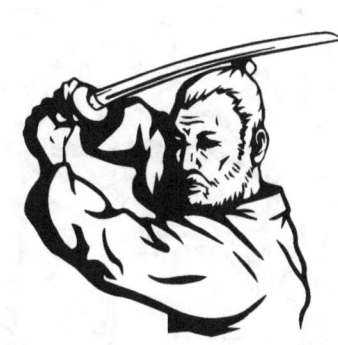

~DEDICATED TO MELOS~

Keep your sword up, and flow like water.

INHALE

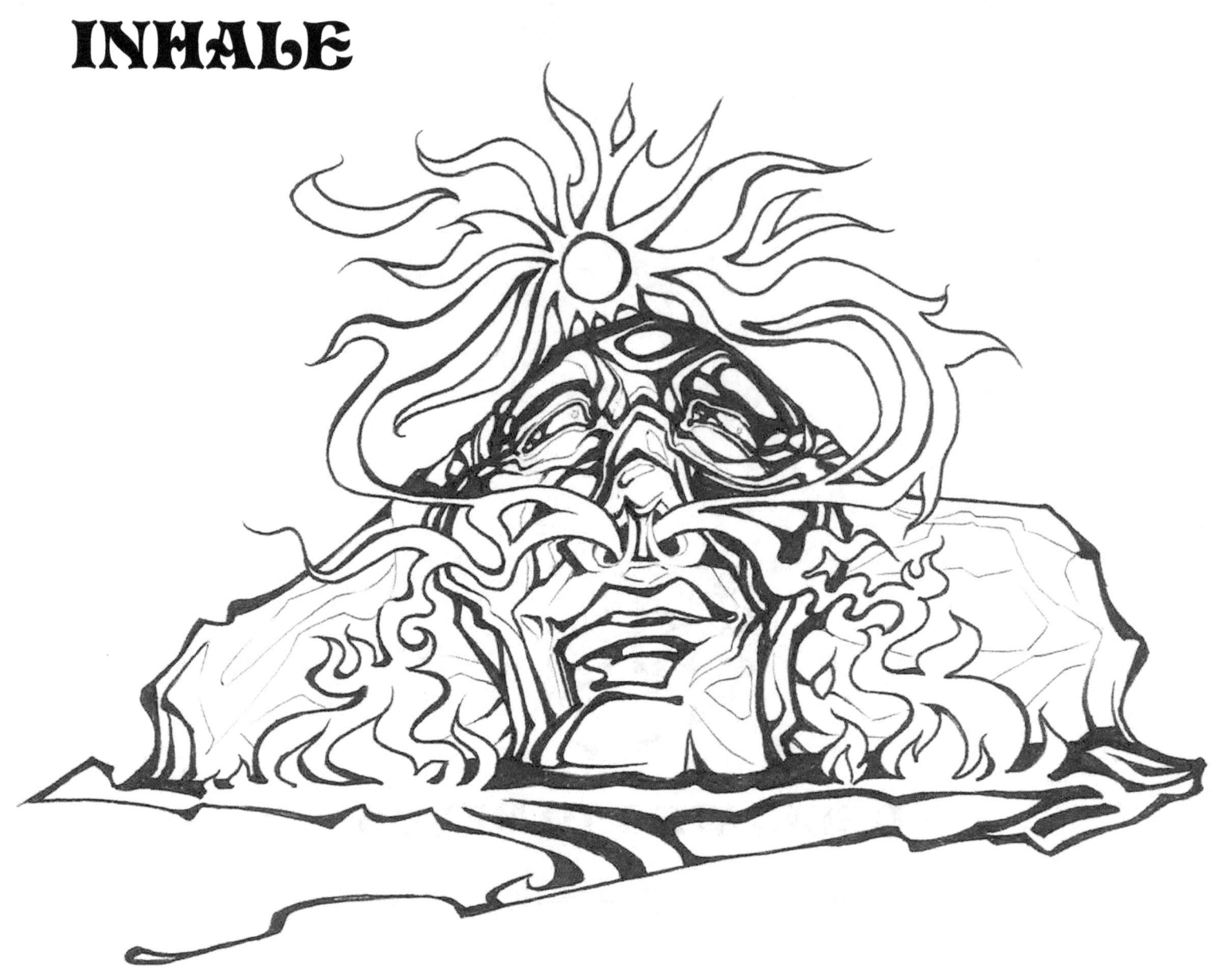

BEFORE YOU BEGIN,

CLOSE YOUR EYES AND SEE THE DARKNESS OF YOUR EYELIDS.

TAKE IN A DEEP BREATH THROUGH YOUR NOSE. THE
BREATH IS FULL OF LIFE.

FEEL THE WARMTH AND COLORS, (YELLOWS, REDS, AND
ORANGE) GO THROUGH YOUR BODY,

ALL THE WAY TO YOUR TOES.

EXHALE

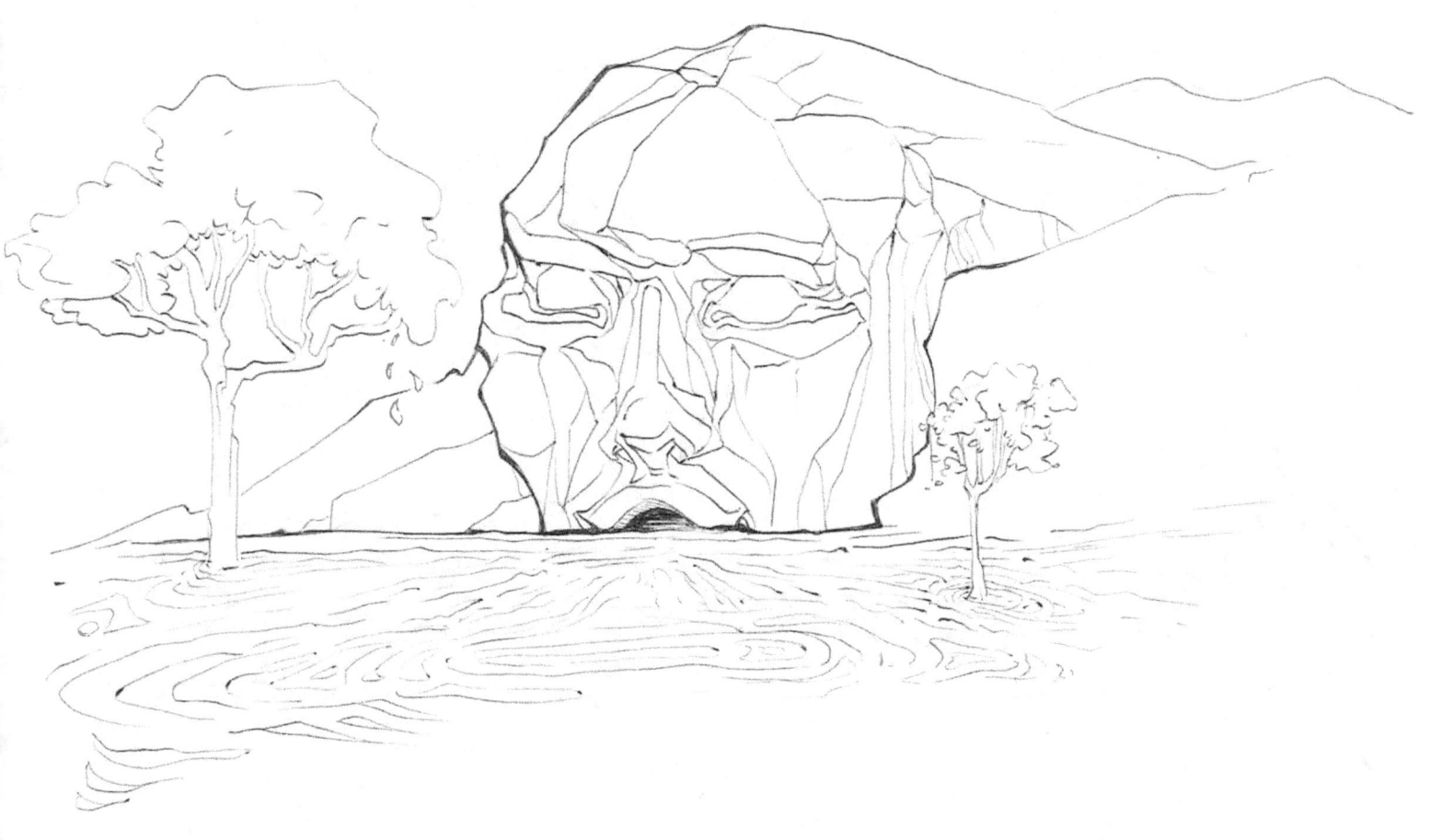

EXHALE OUT THROUGH THE MOUTH AND RELEASE
THE COOL ENERGY, BLUES, GREYS, PURPLE.

TAKE IN MORE COLORFUL AIR THROUGH YOUR NOSE.

EMPTY YOUR MIND AND FOCUS.

THIS IS HOW YOU EVOLVE TO HIGHER LEVELS OF VIBRATION.

EXHALE OUT THE COOL ENERGY.

REPEAT UNTIL YOU ARE READY TO OPEN YOUR EYES
AND TURN THE PAGE.

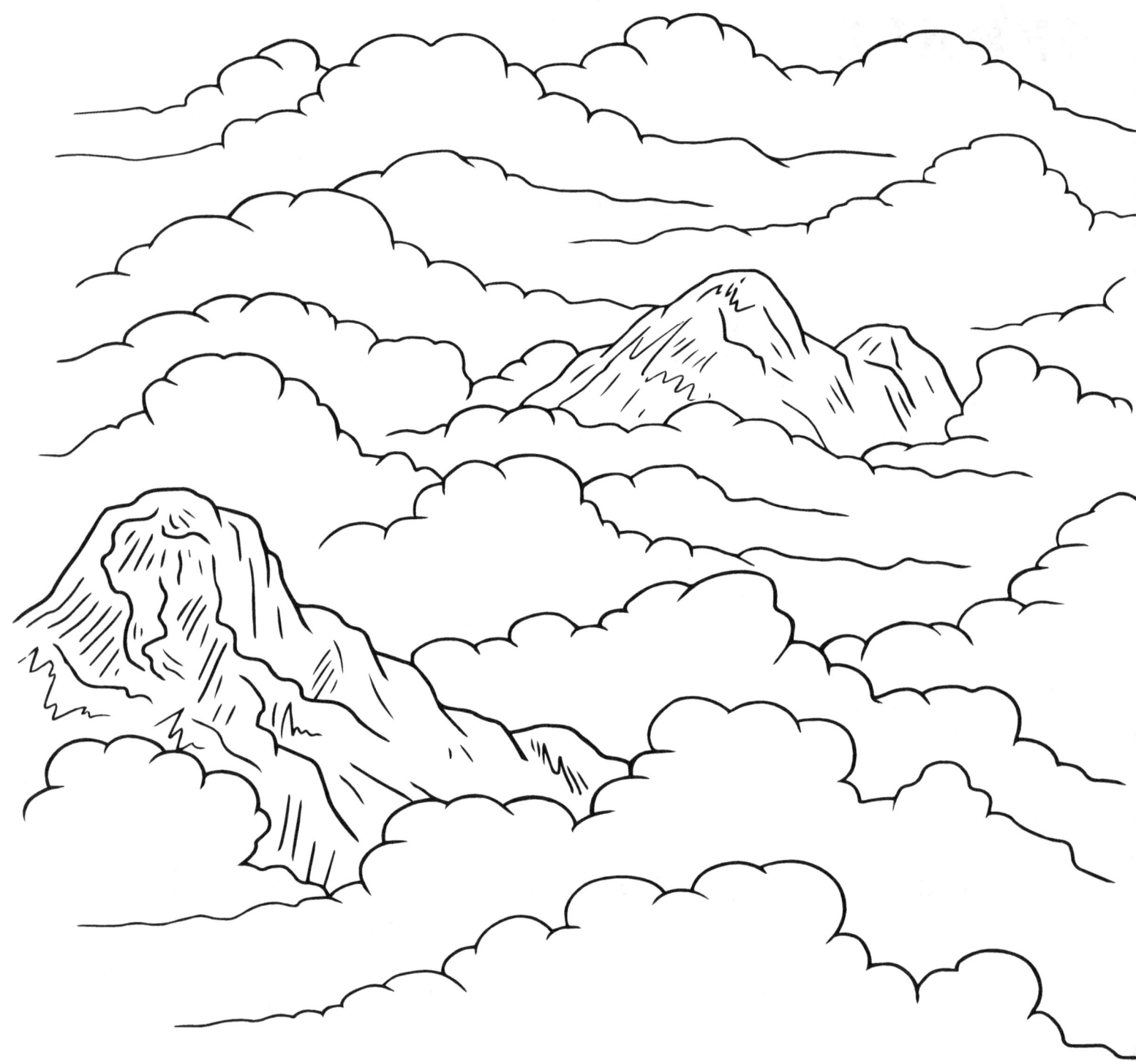

The Mountain

There is a place where East meets West. Where the sunsets and the moon rises on a mountain-top. We make a journey to come take refuge. The lessons on the mountain-top will affect our own light permanently. Through obedience, practice, and patience our light grows, to an understanding of what it is to be a part of the Tribe of Valor. Equipping us to go out into the world, and help others with healing arts.

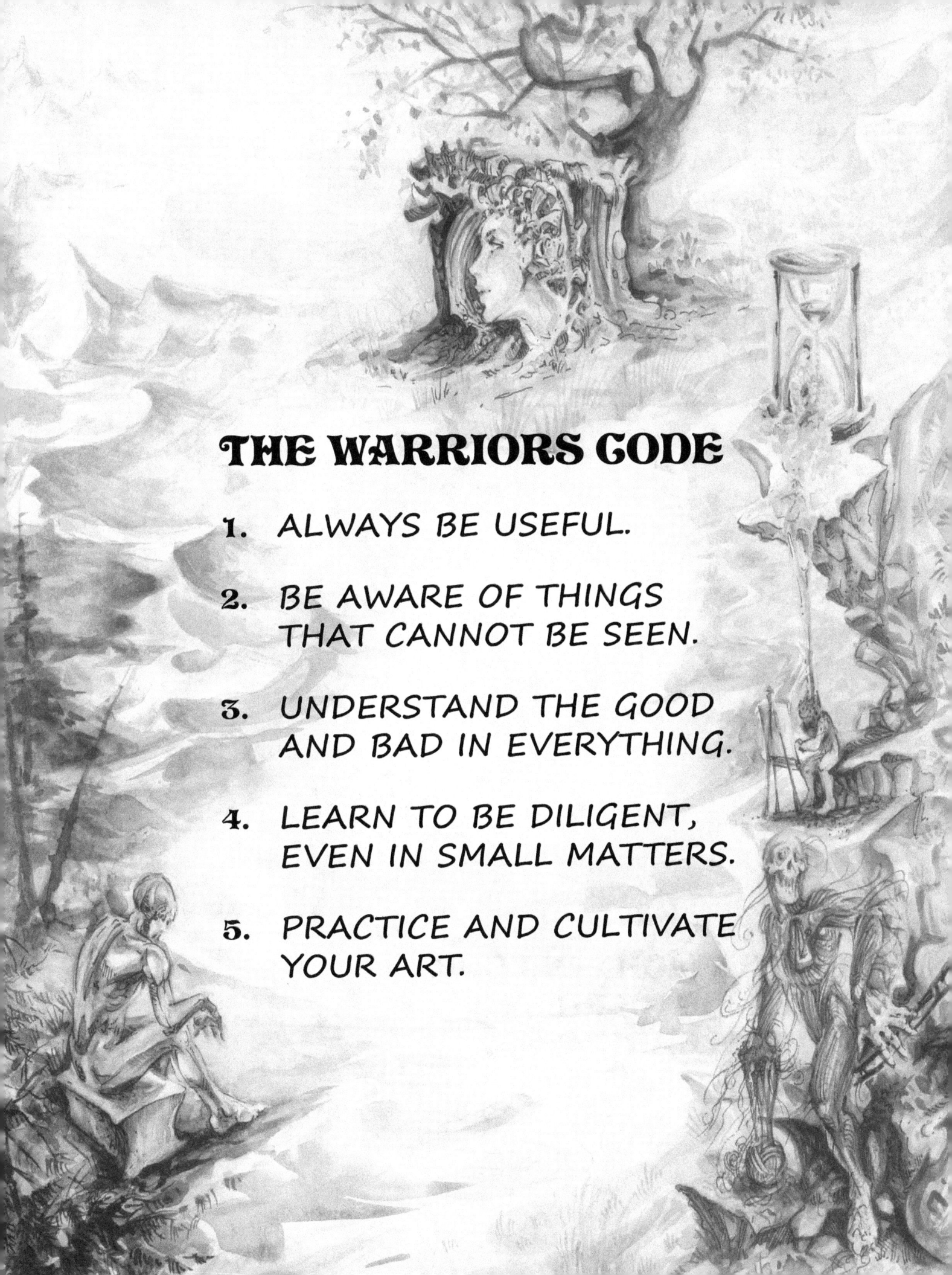

THE WARRIORS CODE

1. ALWAYS BE USEFUL.

2. BE AWARE OF THINGS
    THAT CANNOT BE SEEN.

3. UNDERSTAND THE GOOD
    AND BAD IN EVERYTHING.

4. LEARN TO BE DILIGENT,
    EVEN IN SMALL MATTERS.

5. PRACTICE AND CULTIVATE
    YOUR ART.

The eye is a lamp that provides light for the body. When the eye is good, the whole body is filled with light. When the light is bad the whole body is filled with darkness. If you are not open to receive the light, you will have denial. Denial does not allow the light in.

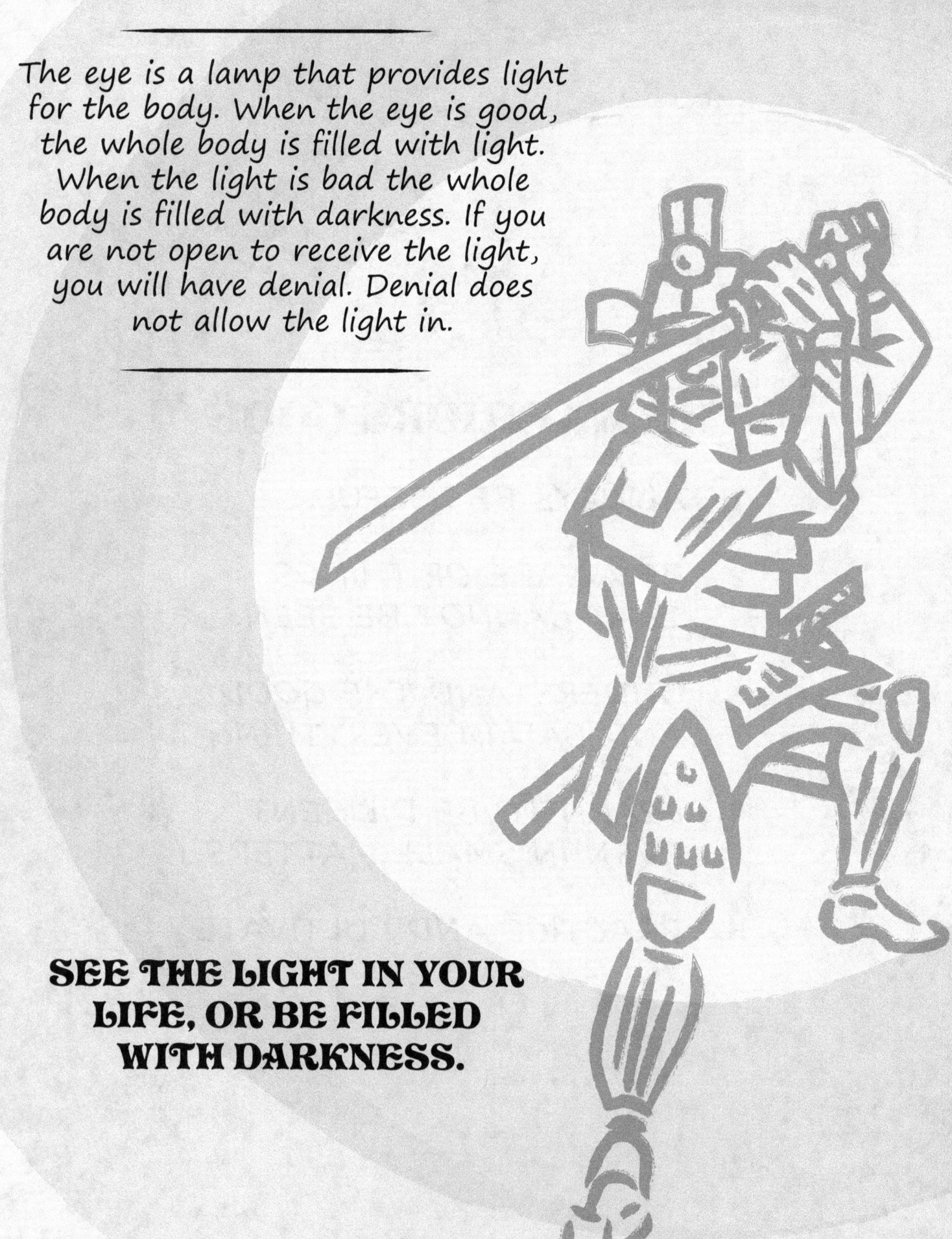

SEE THE LIGHT IN YOUR LIFE, OR BE FILLED WITH DARKNESS.

~ ALL OF CREATION WILL BE SHAKEN, SO THAT ONLY UNSHAKABLE THINGS WILL REMAIN.

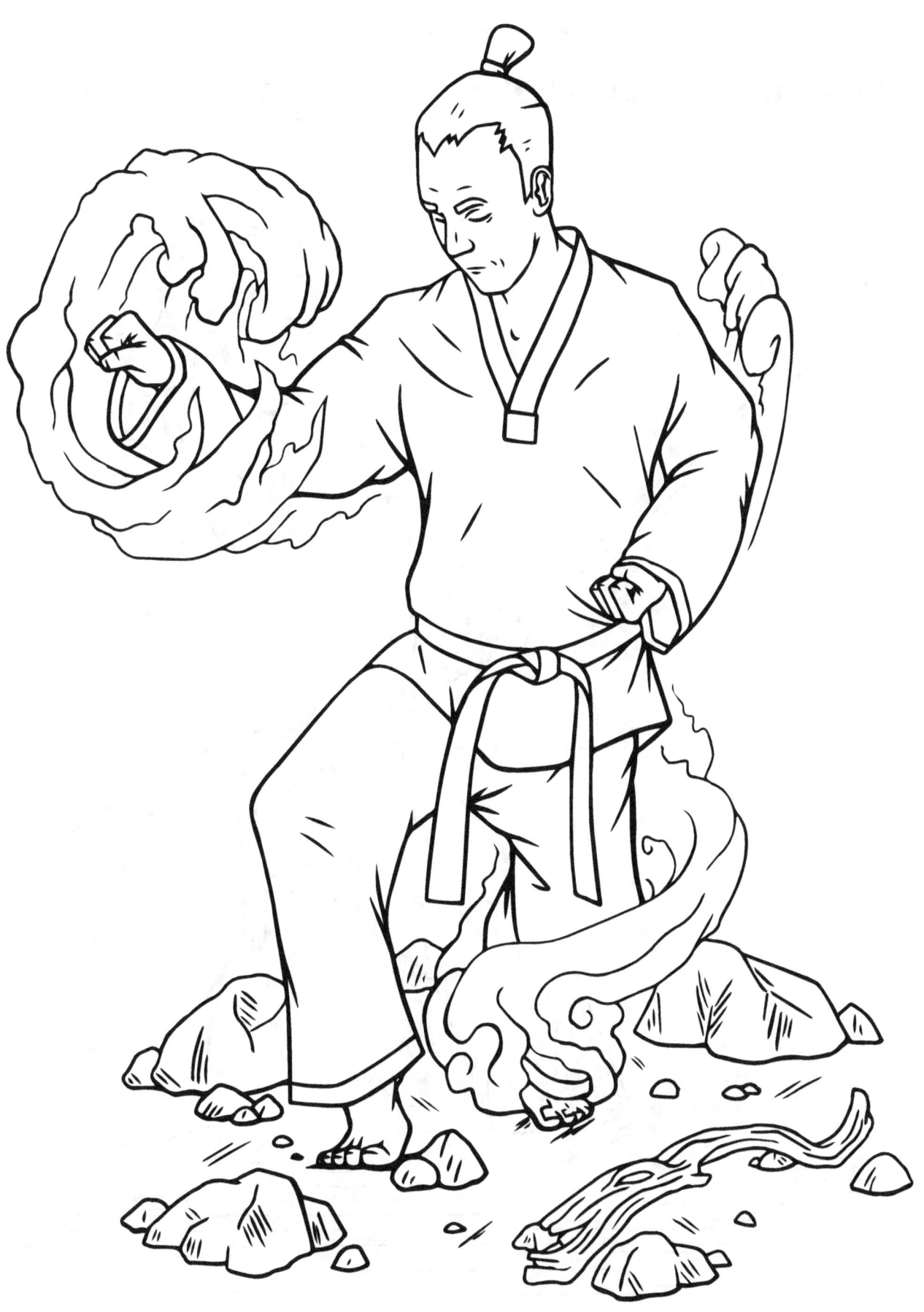

DON'T WORRY ABOUT TOMORROW FOR TOMORROW
WILL BRING ON ITS OWN WORRIES. TODAYS
TROUBLES ARE ENOUGH FOR TODAY.

WE ARE NEVER GIVEN MORE THAN WE CAN HANDLE.

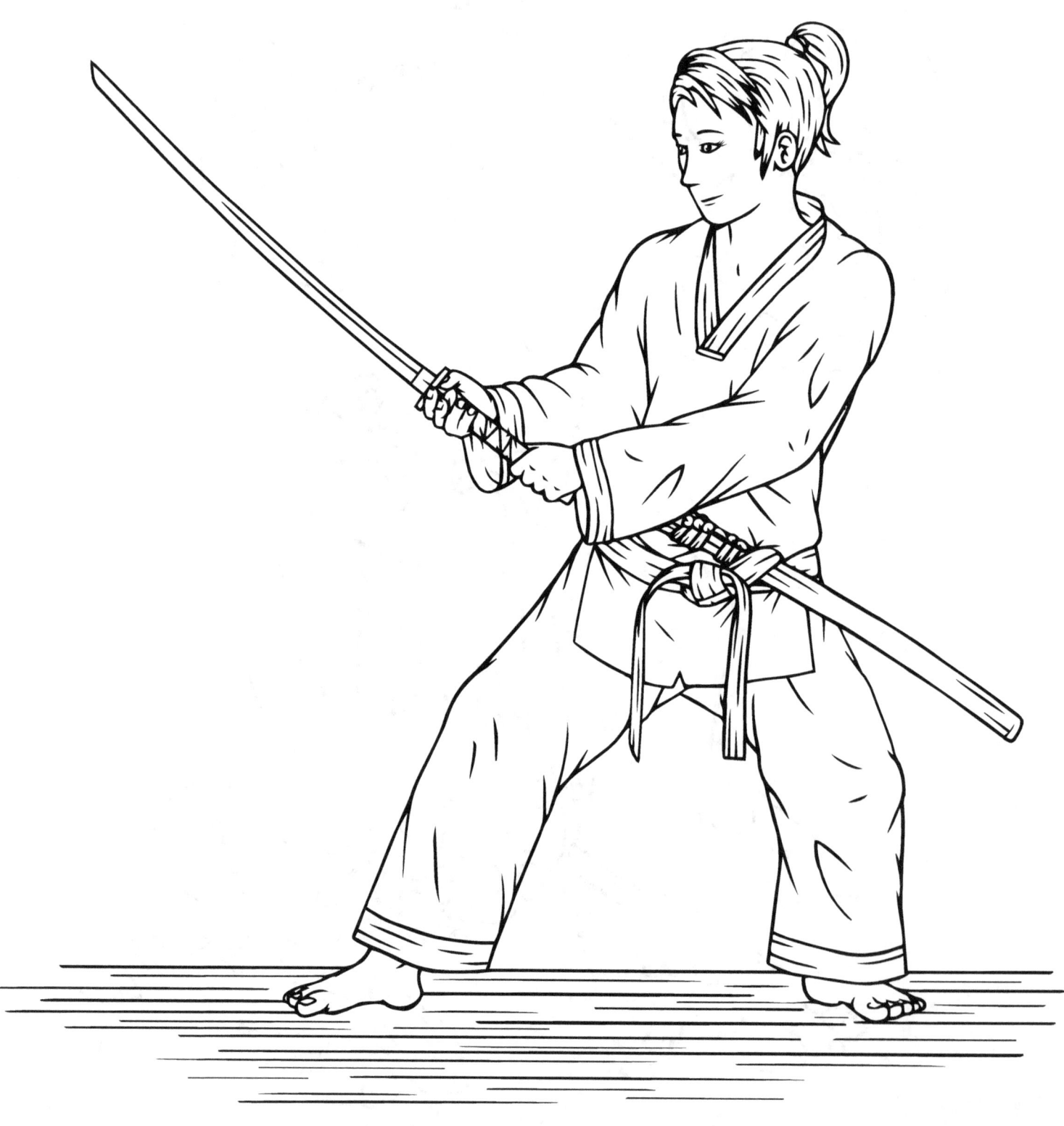

No discipline is enjoyable in the moment, but afterward there will be a peaceful harvest of right living for those who are trained in this practiced way.

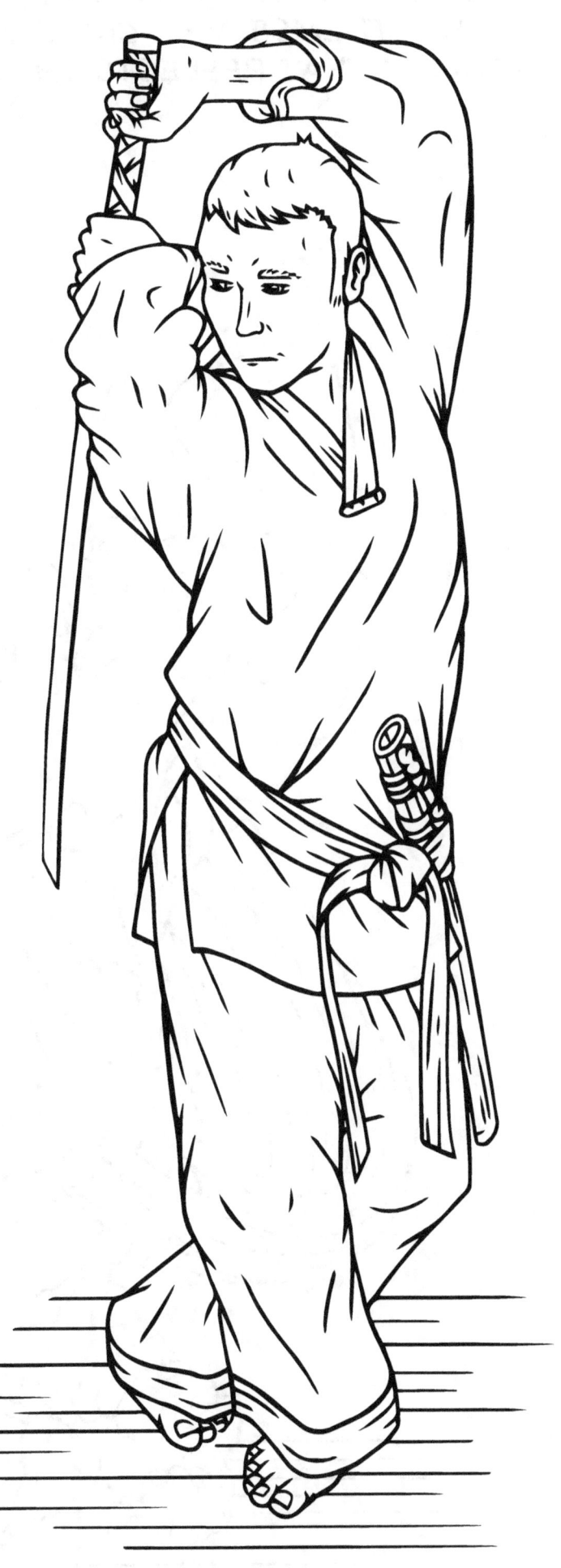

EACH WARRIOR HAS A CONFLICT TO RESOLVE
WITHIN THEMSELVES, CREATING AN OUTER
REALITY THAT REFLECTS THIS.

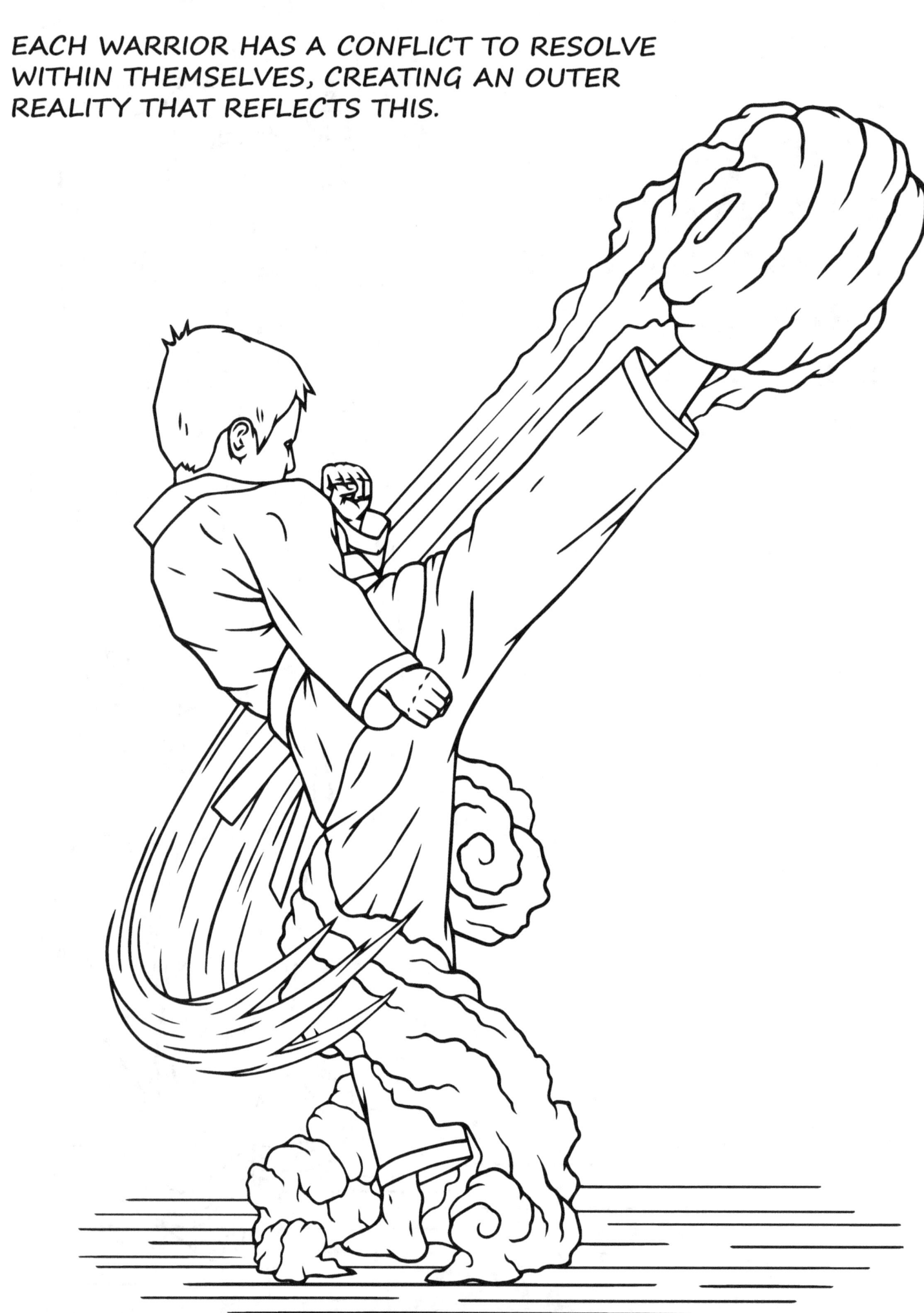

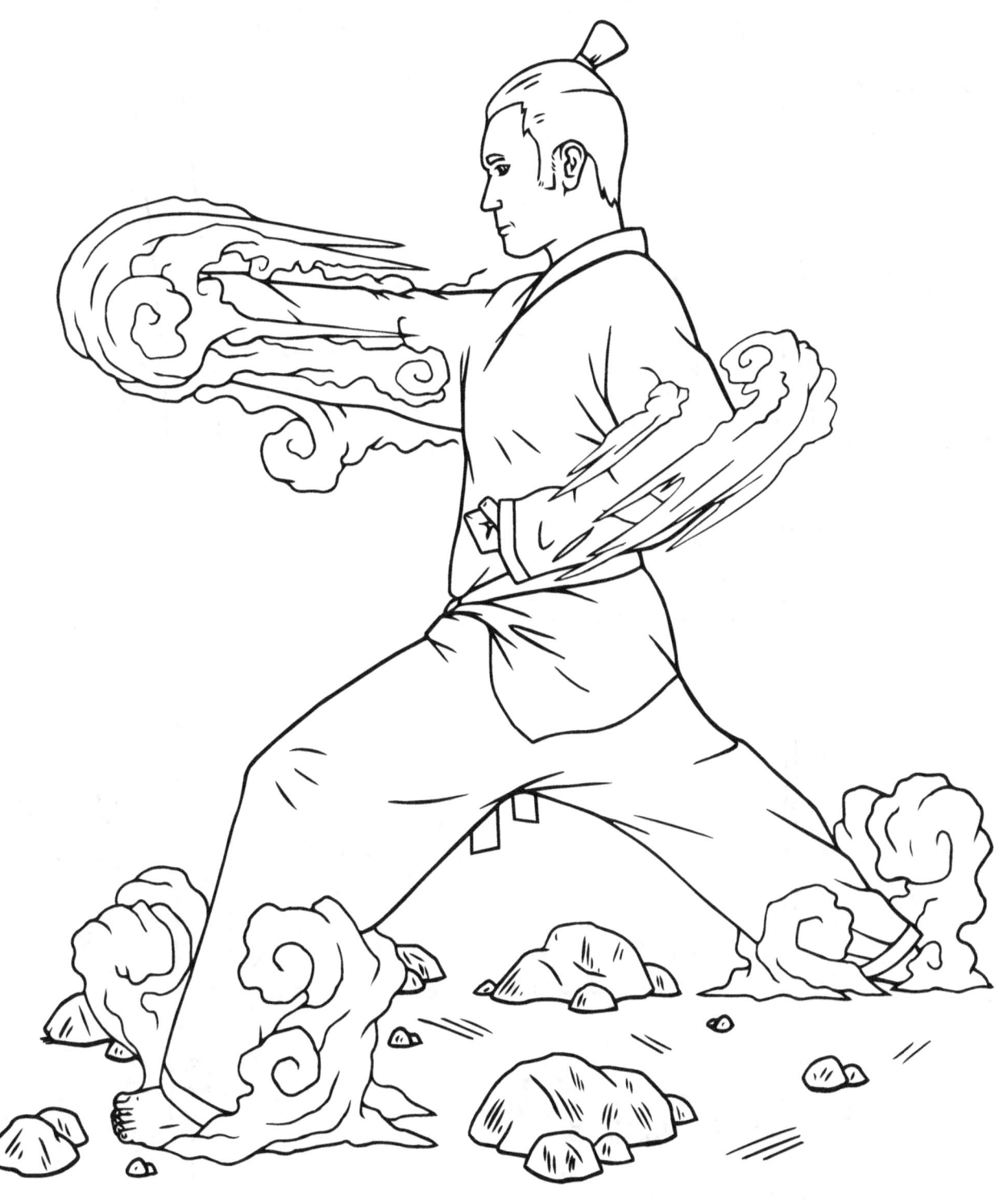

"Among the most important personal choices you can make is to accept complete responsibility for everything you are and everything you will ever be. The acceptance of personal responsibility is what separates the superior person from the average person."

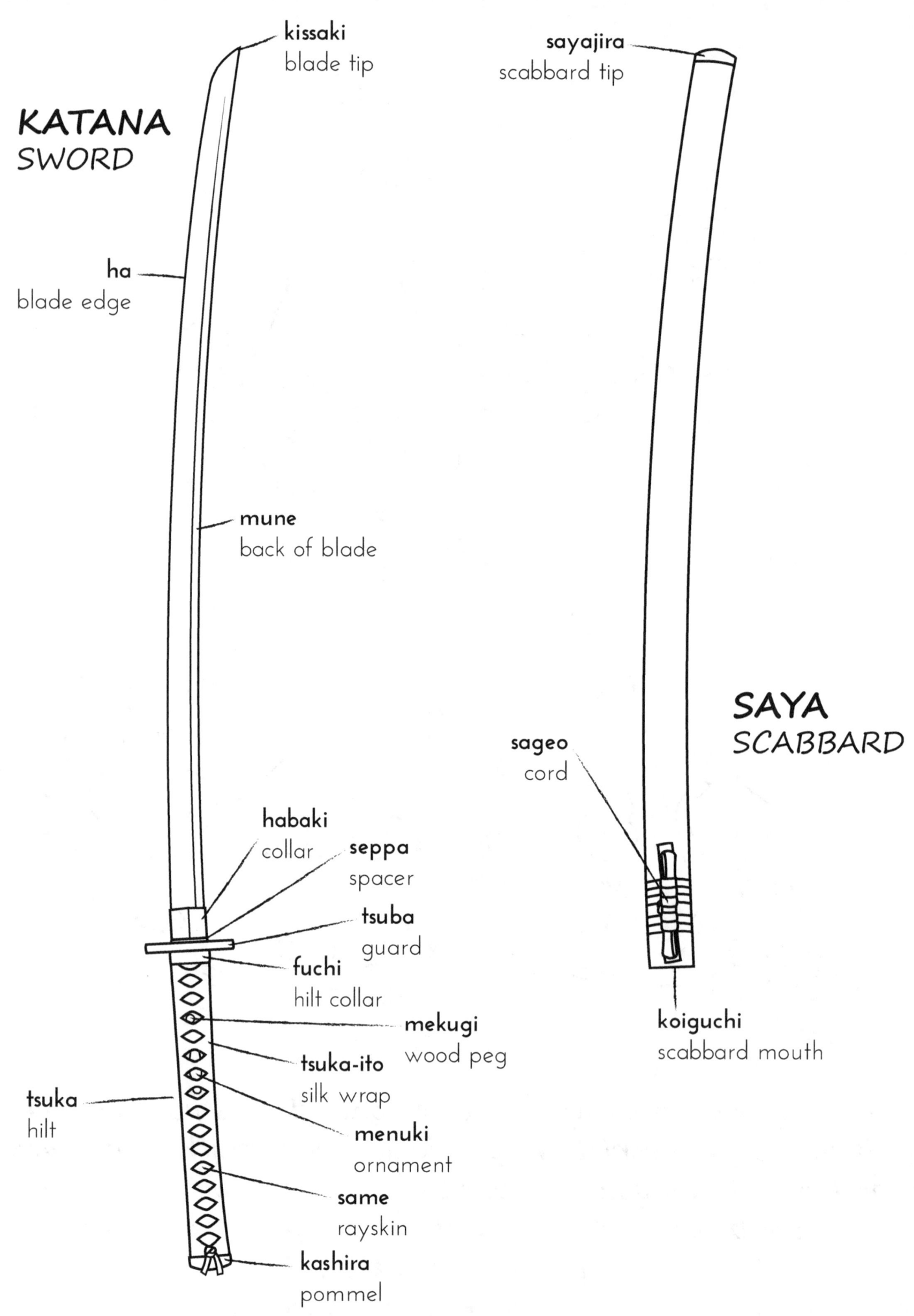

kissaki
blade tip

KATANA
SWORD

sayajira
scabbard tip

ha
blade edge

mune
back of blade

SAYA
SCABBARD

sageo
cord

habaki
collar

seppa
spacer

tsuba
guard

fuchi
hilt collar

mekugi
wood peg

tsuka-ito
silk wrap

menuki
ornament

same
rayskin

kashira
pommel

tsuka
hilt

koiguchi
scabbard mouth

SWORD CROSSWORD PUZZLE

WRITE IN THE JAPANESE SWORD TERMS USING THE PICTURE

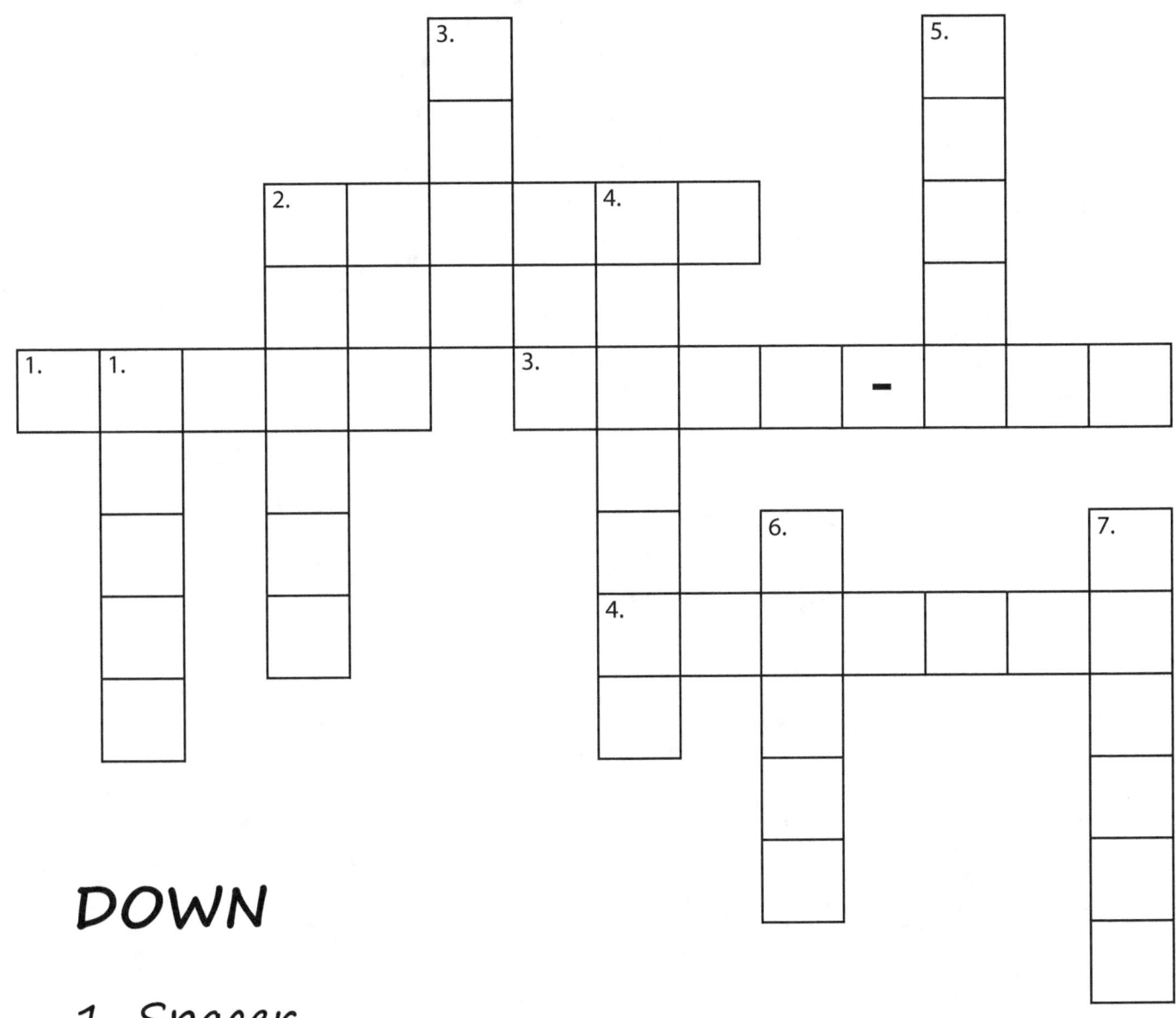

DOWN

1. Spacer
2. Wood Peg
3. Back of Blade
4. Blade Tip
5. Hilt Collar
6. Guard
7. Collar

ACROSS

1. Hilt
2. Ornament
3. Silk Wrap
4. Pommel

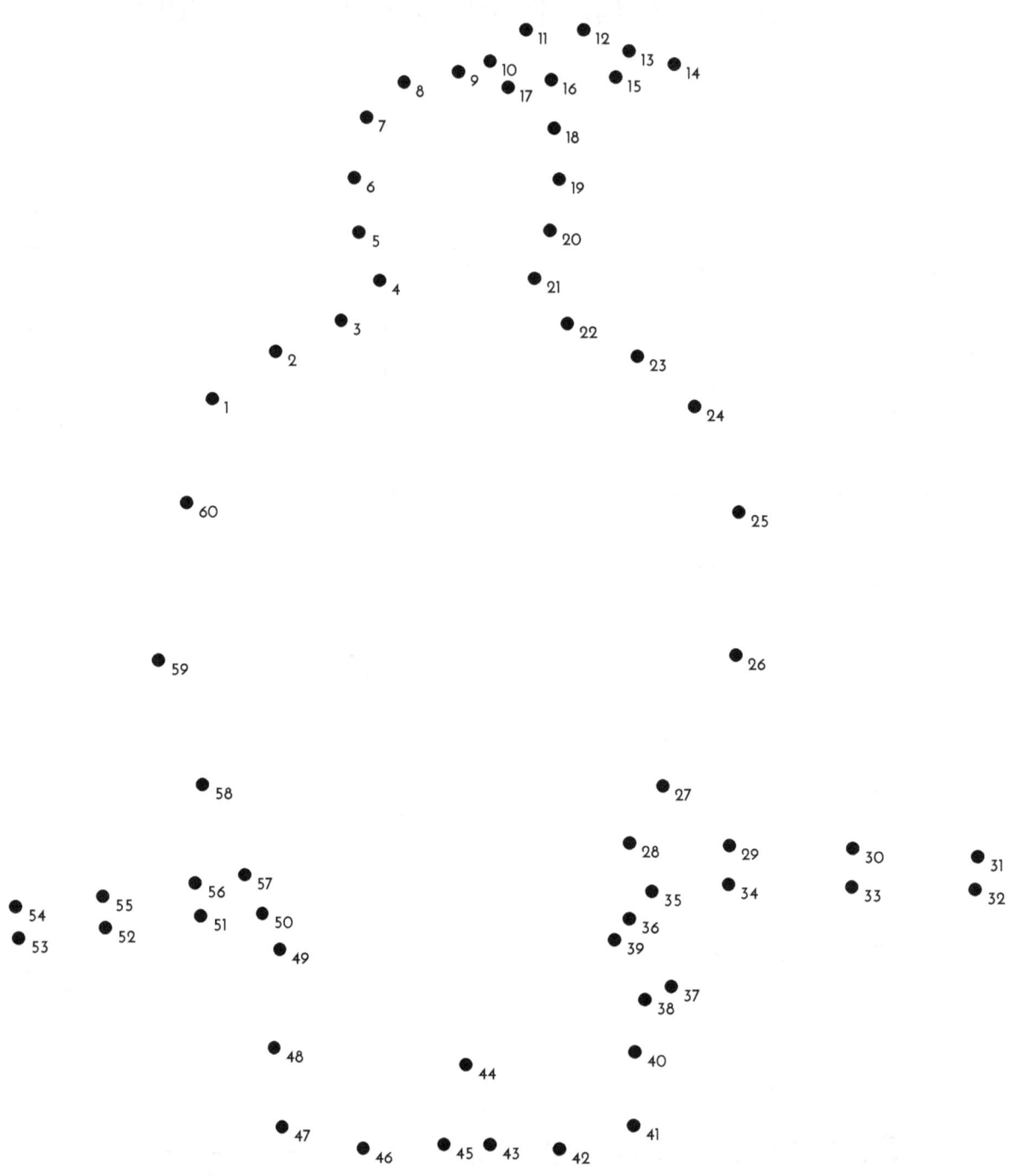

We have the ability to create our own reality through thought and actions. When we create, it is called the imagination. Imagination is an idea or mental picture in the mind.

VISUALIZE YOURSELF AT A HIGHER STATE OF BEING AND LIVE THE MOST FULFILLING LIFE YOU CAN IMAGINE EVERYDAY.

EVERYONE WILL BE TESTED WITH FIRE.

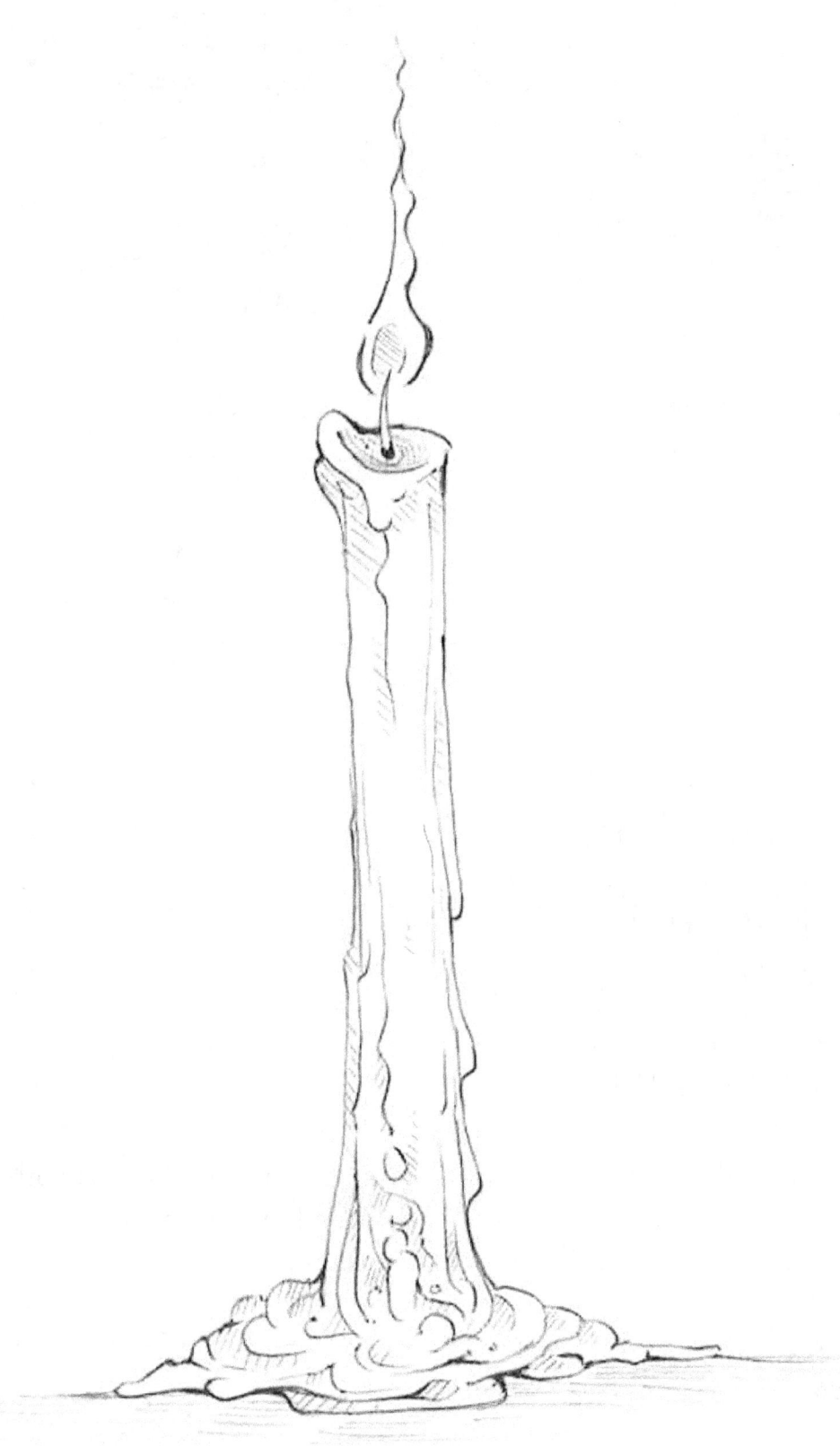

WHAT HAS LIGHT MUST ENDURE BURNING.

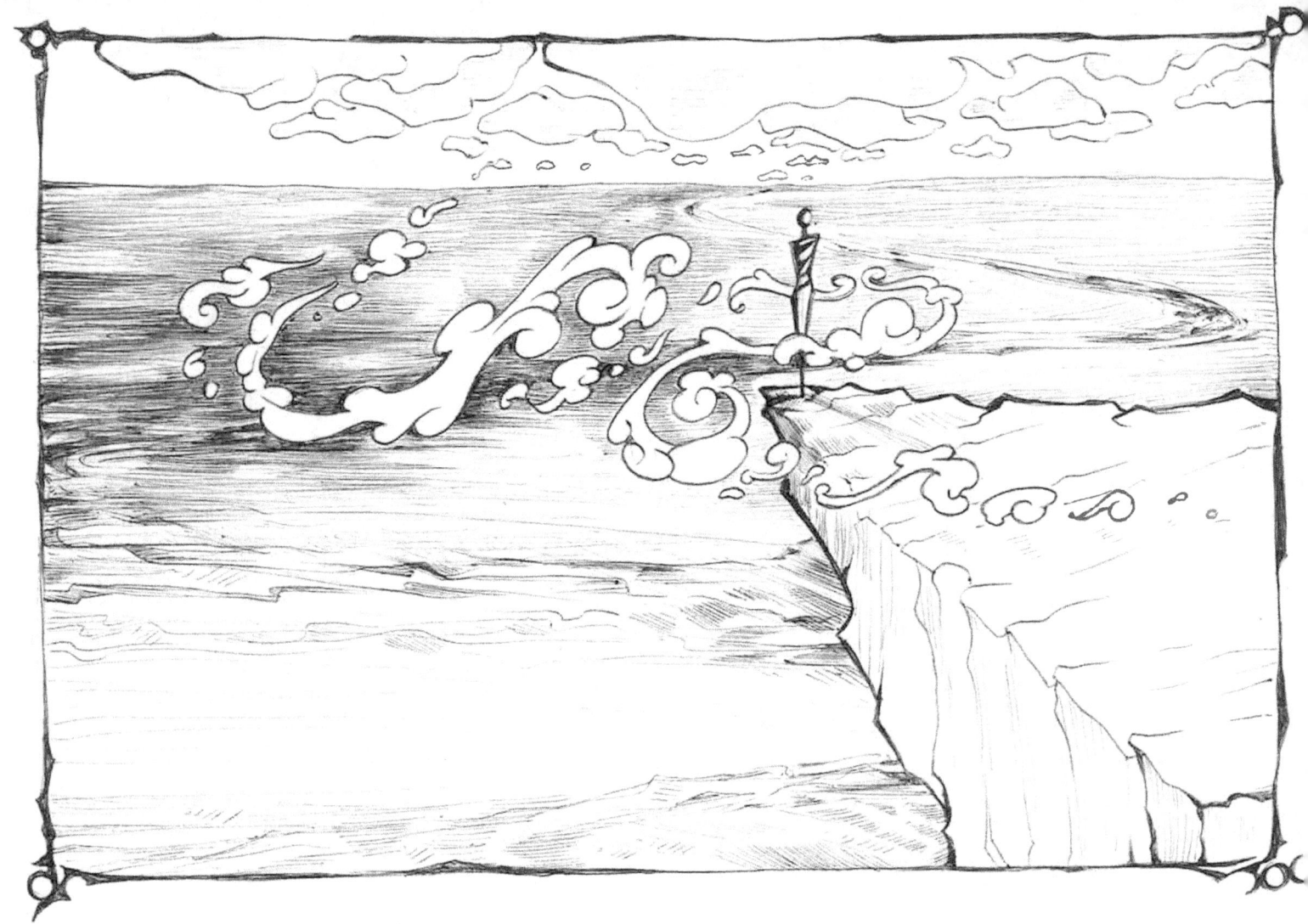

WAKING UP EACH DAY =	70 points
POSITIVE/NEGATIVE THOUGHT =	5/-5 points
POSITIVE/NEGATIVE ACTION=	10/-10 points
POSITIVE/NEGATIVE THOUGHT+ACTION	25/-25 points
STAYING POSITIVE=	10 points
TURNING A NEGATIVE TO A POSITIVE=	50 points
MOVING PAST NEGATIVITY=	10 points
ATTITUDE OF GRATITUDE=	10 points

1. We are born with 50 percent of our happiness in our DNA. Another 10 percent is determined by outside circumstances. And the other 40 percent is determined by our attitude and reaction toward those circumstances.

2. We start each day with a fresh 70 points. At the end of the day, before you go to bed, evaluate your day and score yourself.

If you score 120 points or higher, journal about your day.

ART OF LIVING

There is an Artist who spends a lifetime working on a portrait. The Artist has learned that what is being created is permanent and will never be perfect. The Artist continually defines the portrait through circumstance and experience. The Artist has earned the culmination of the work on the portrait up to this point. The Artist's work is never done.

What motivates the Artist to create? What will the Artist do when the portrait is complete? Will The Artist appreciate the creation or the creator? The portrait is not easy, it takes time and energy to build and create. At times, The Artist questions the very existence of the portrait and the power to create it...

Through the growing pains, The Artist has found that what has been created is not for their pleasure alone. Overcoming fears and insecurities will define the portrait. The Artist surrounded the portrait with a wall of righteousness, with the integrity to withstand forever. Wisdom and understanding are the tools learned to edify and strengthen because The Artist's foundation is love and truth. The portrait shows layers of overcoming adversity. The power to create is destiny. When the Artist finds the meaning and the value of the portrait, the journey will be complete. The signature marks the legacy code that personalizes the portrait.

The Artist is living art and the portrait of time is the masterpiece.

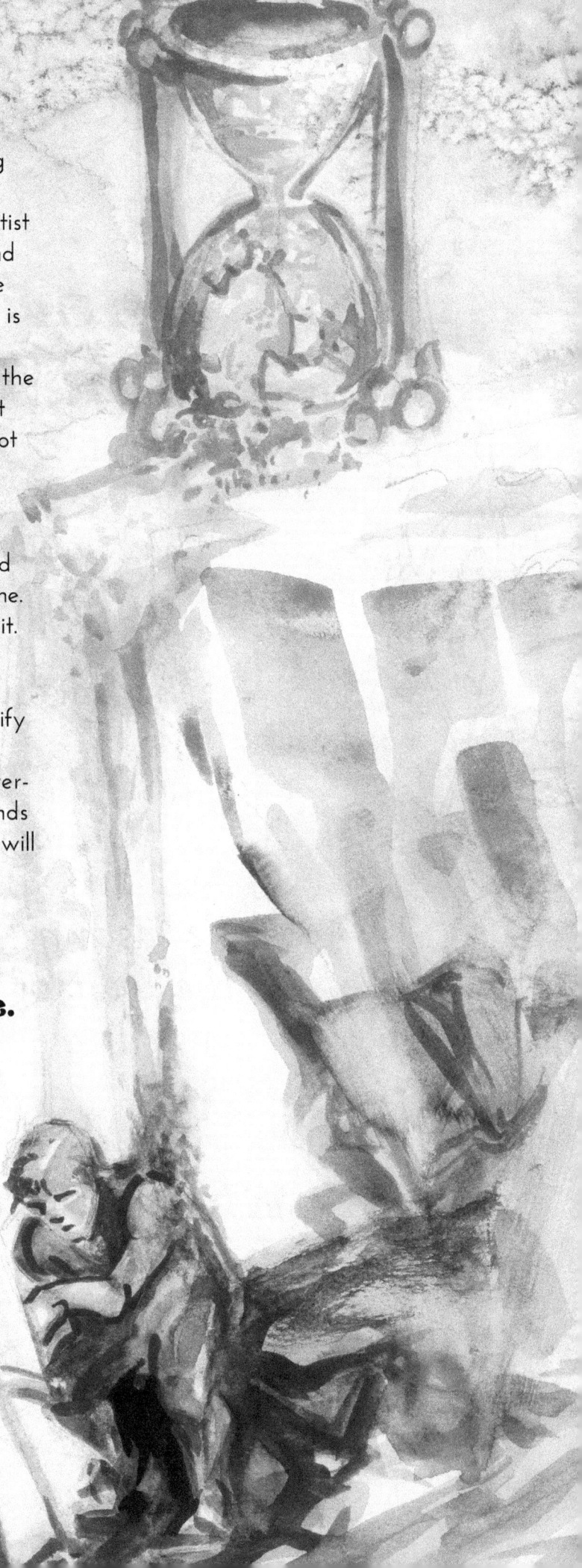

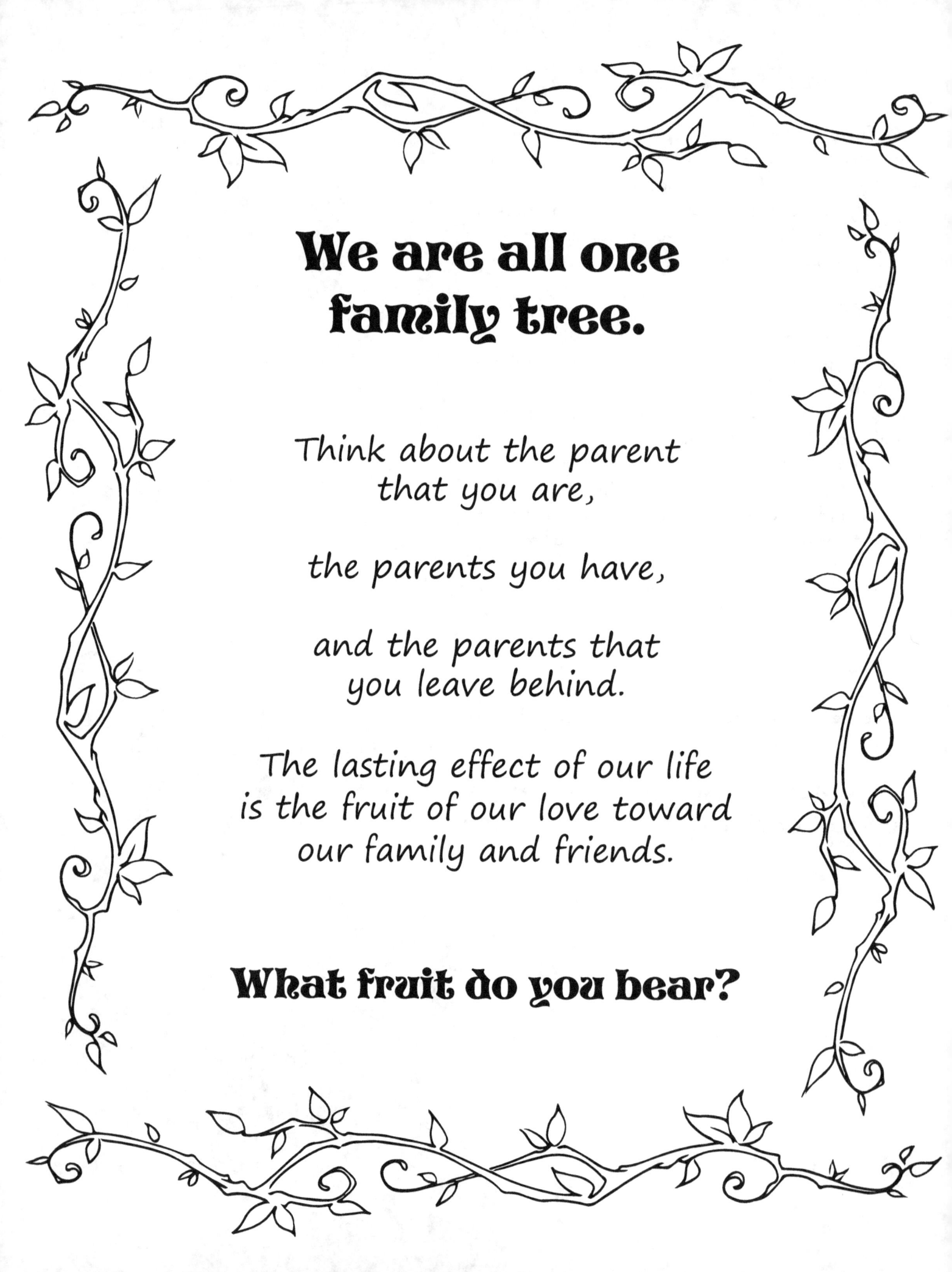

We are all one family tree.

Think about the parent
that you are,

the parents you have,

and the parents that
you leave behind.

The lasting effect of our life
is the fruit of our love toward
our family and friends.

What fruit do you bear?

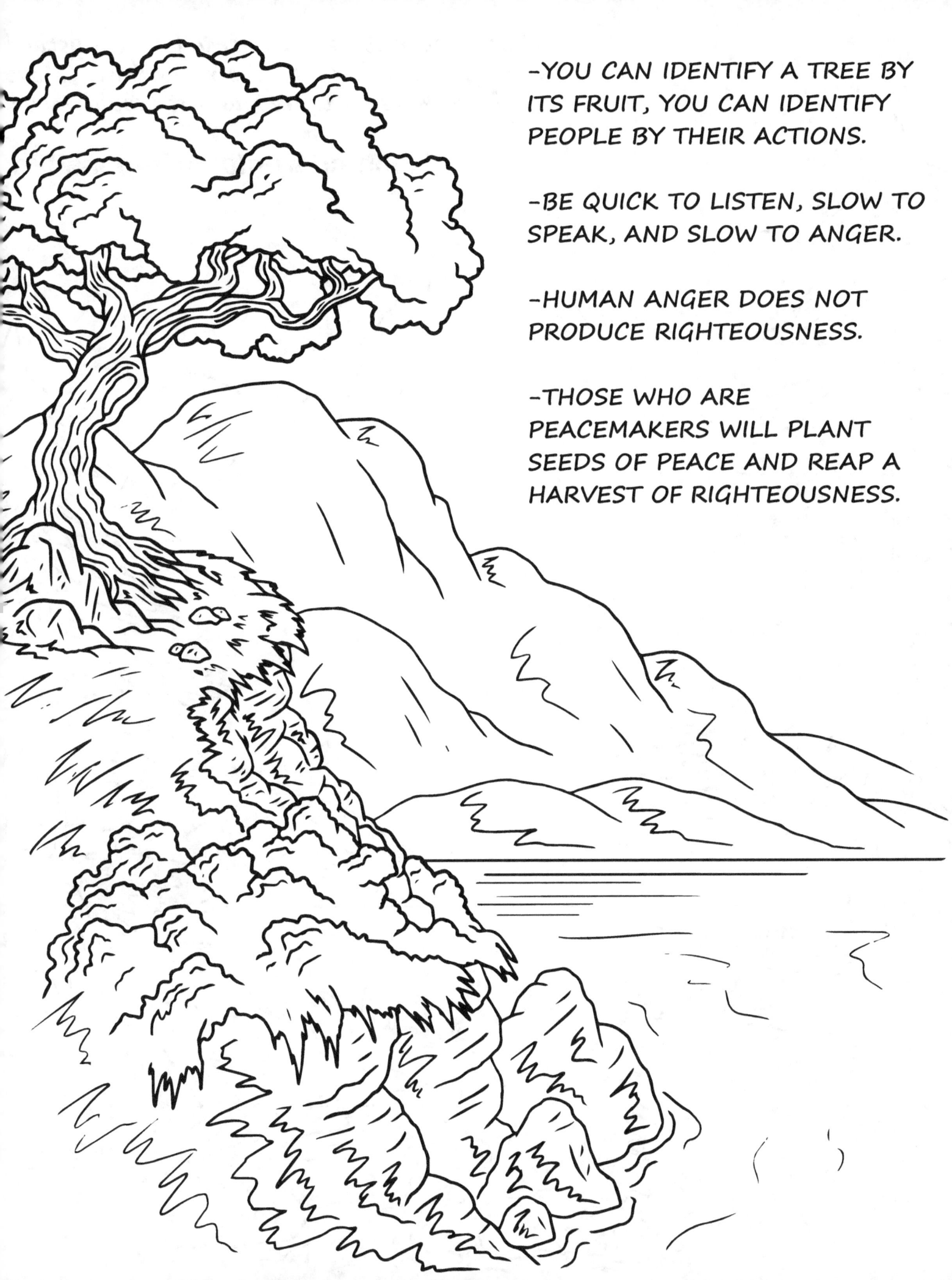

-YOU CAN IDENTIFY A TREE BY ITS FRUIT, YOU CAN IDENTIFY PEOPLE BY THEIR ACTIONS.

-BE QUICK TO LISTEN, SLOW TO SPEAK, AND SLOW TO ANGER.

-HUMAN ANGER DOES NOT PRODUCE RIGHTEOUSNESS.

-THOSE WHO ARE PEACEMAKERS WILL PLANT SEEDS OF PEACE AND REAP A HARVEST OF RIGHTEOUSNESS.

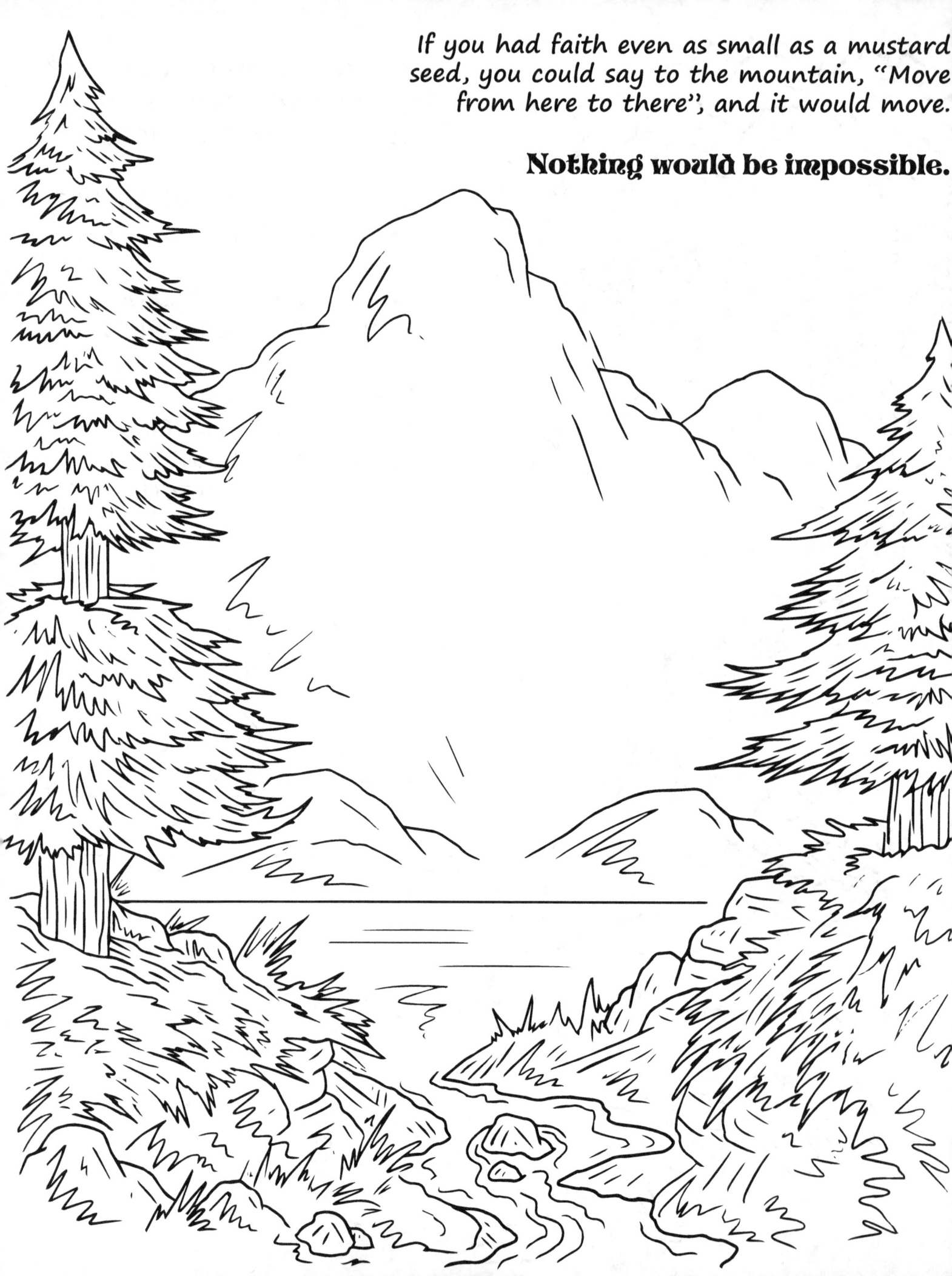

If you had faith even as small as a mustard seed, you could say to the mountain, "Move from here to there", and it would move.

Nothing would be impossible.

The Master is the one who continues down the path day after day, year after year.

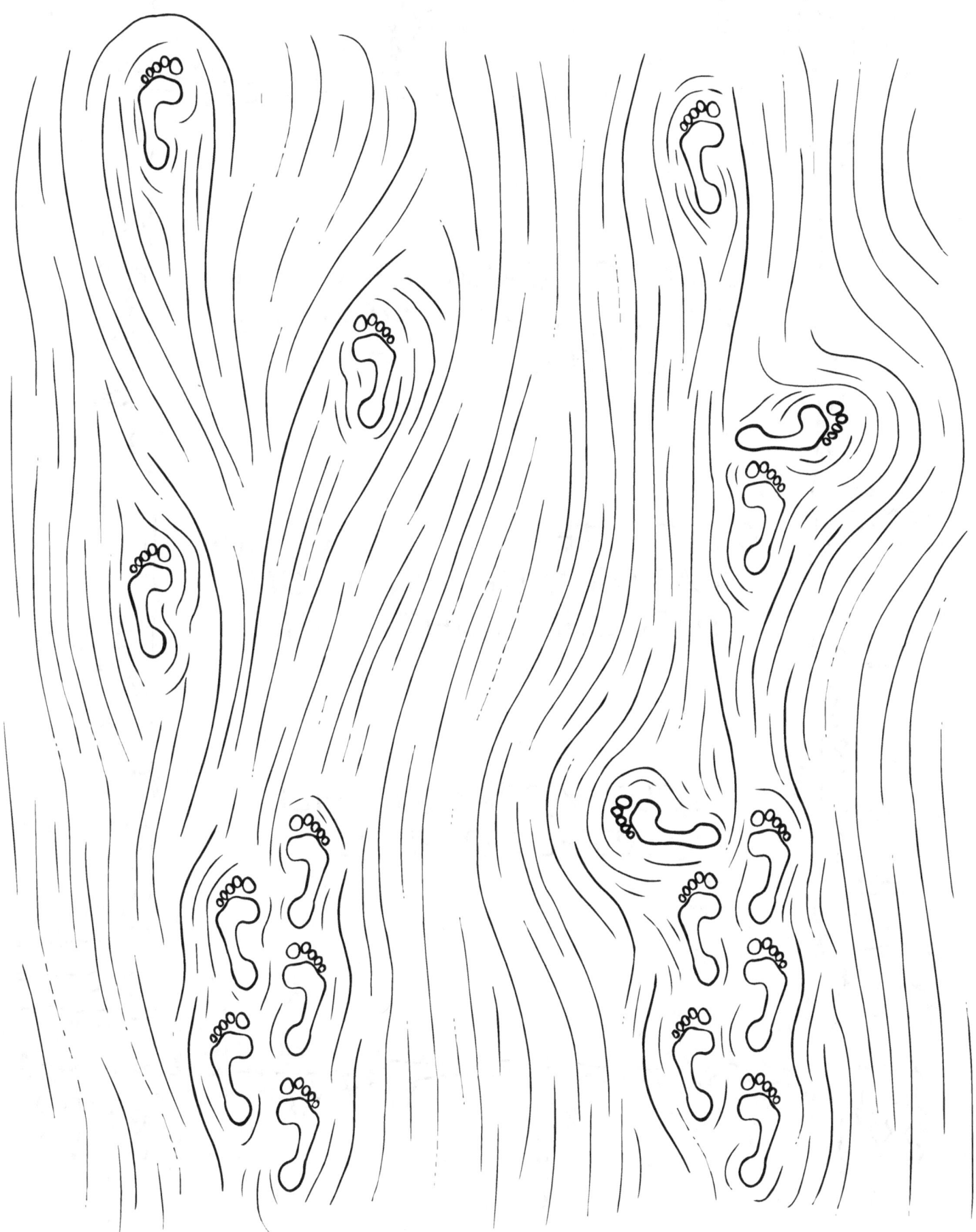

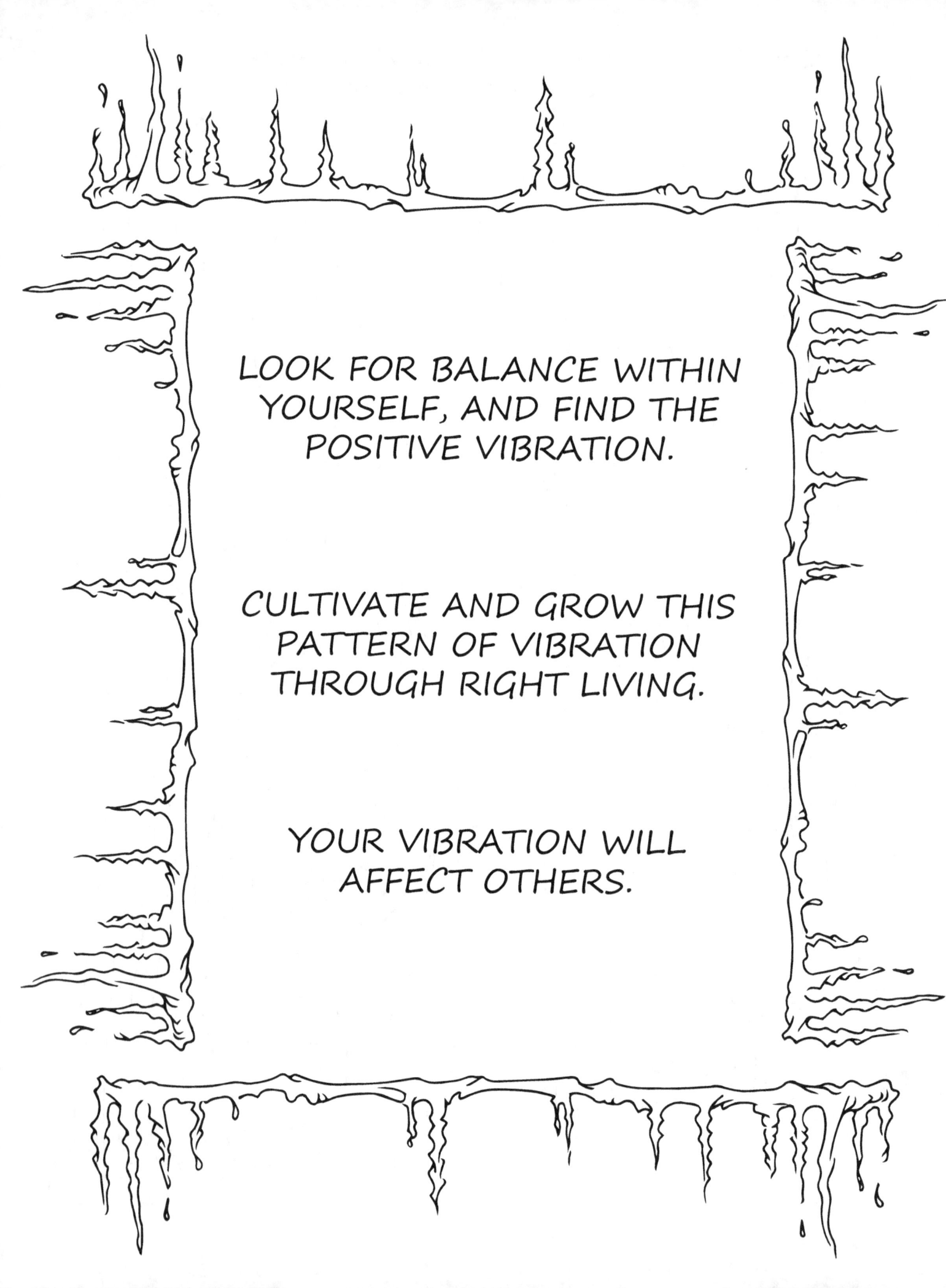

LOOK FOR BALANCE WITHIN
YOURSELF, AND FIND THE
POSITIVE VIBRATION.

CULTIVATE AND GROW THIS
PATTERN OF VIBRATION
THROUGH RIGHT LIVING.

YOUR VIBRATION WILL
AFFECT OTHERS.

THE BATTLE OF THE TWO WOLVES

There are two wolves that live inside us all.

One is Unhappiness.
It is fear, worry, anger, jealousy, sorrow, hate, resentment and inferiority.

One is Happiness.
It is joy, love, hope, serenity, kindness, generosity, truth and compassion.

Which wolf wins the battle?

THE ONE YOU FEED.

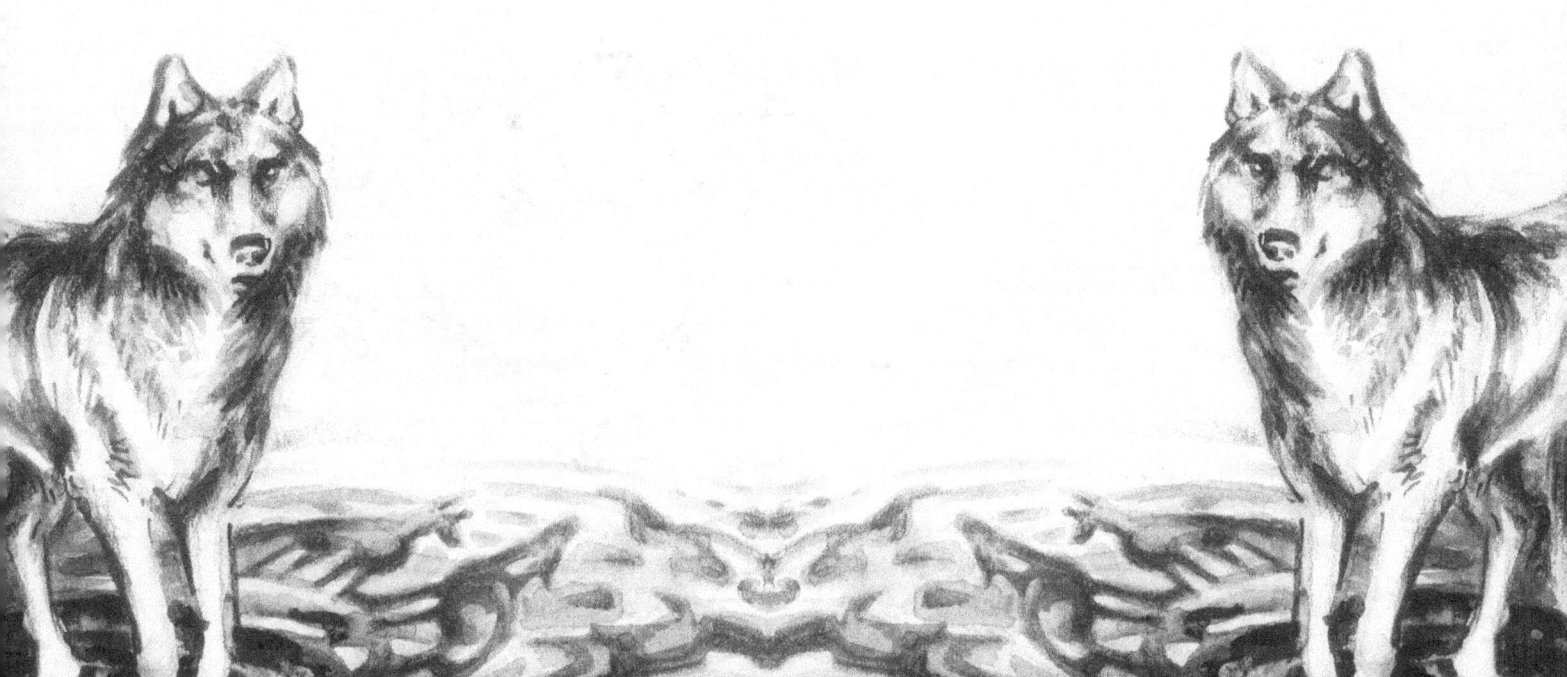

The Mountain Called Life

I am climbing a mountain called life. The mountain of life brings change and sometimes it is a struggle to keep climbing day after day. However I am the river that perseveres through the mountain. I will not give up! Persistence on my portrait has made me a Master.

I am not limited to boundaries. Being open to new experiences with a willingness to try is how I overcome my fears. I am climbing the mountain of life in search for the Truth. This is a committed journey of patience, practice, self discovery, and respect. The true gift is waiting at the top of the mountain. I can't tell you what it is because you have to search that out on your own. I want to encourage you to keep pushing toward your perfection.

When you get to the top of the mountain, take in the fresh air. Watch the sky fall down to the earth. Now stop watching and start seeing. Seeing comes from the heart. See with the eyes of the mountain. See the layers, and the process of time that it takes to get to the top. The success on the mountain is not by chance. If you follow the Truth it will get you where you need to go.

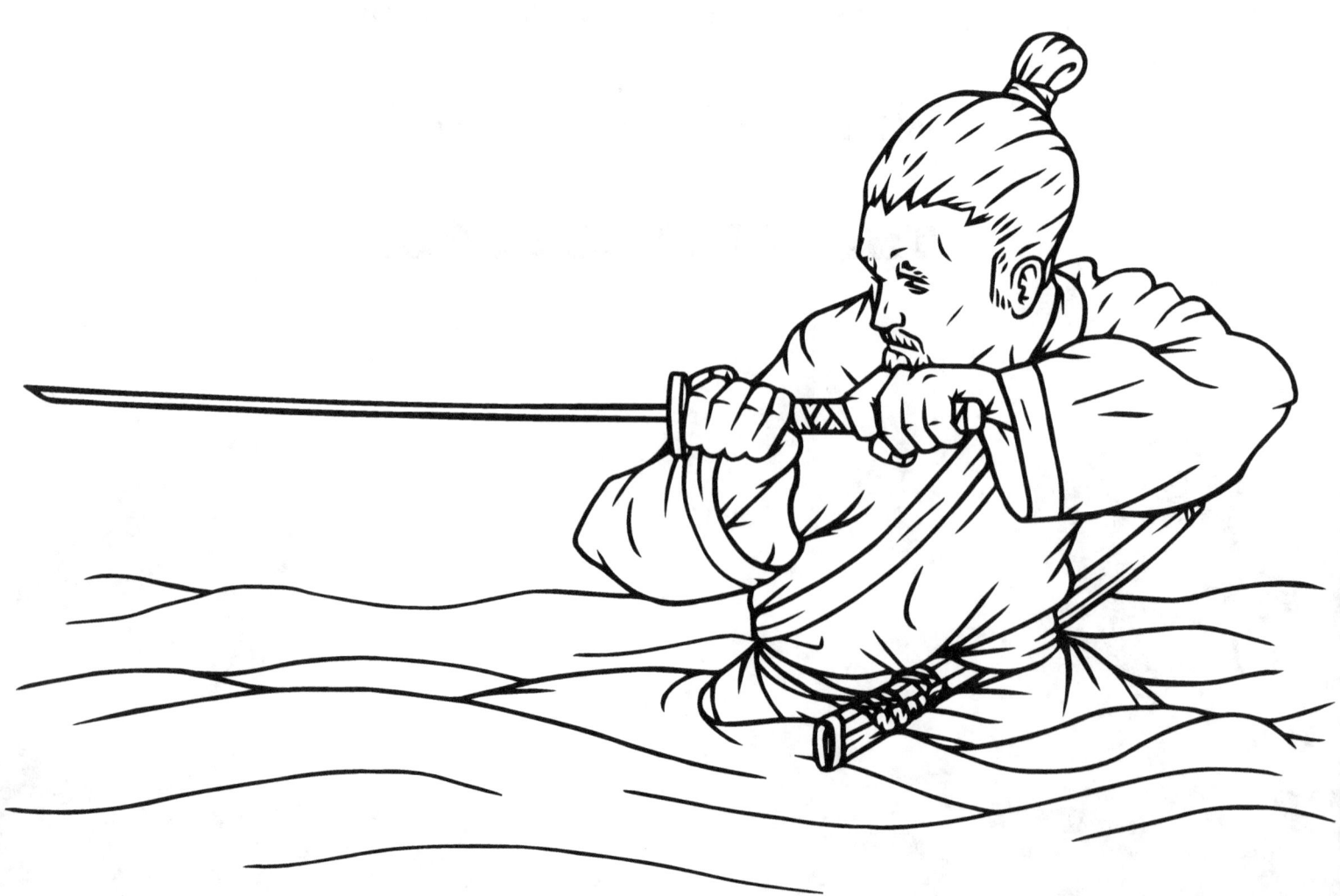

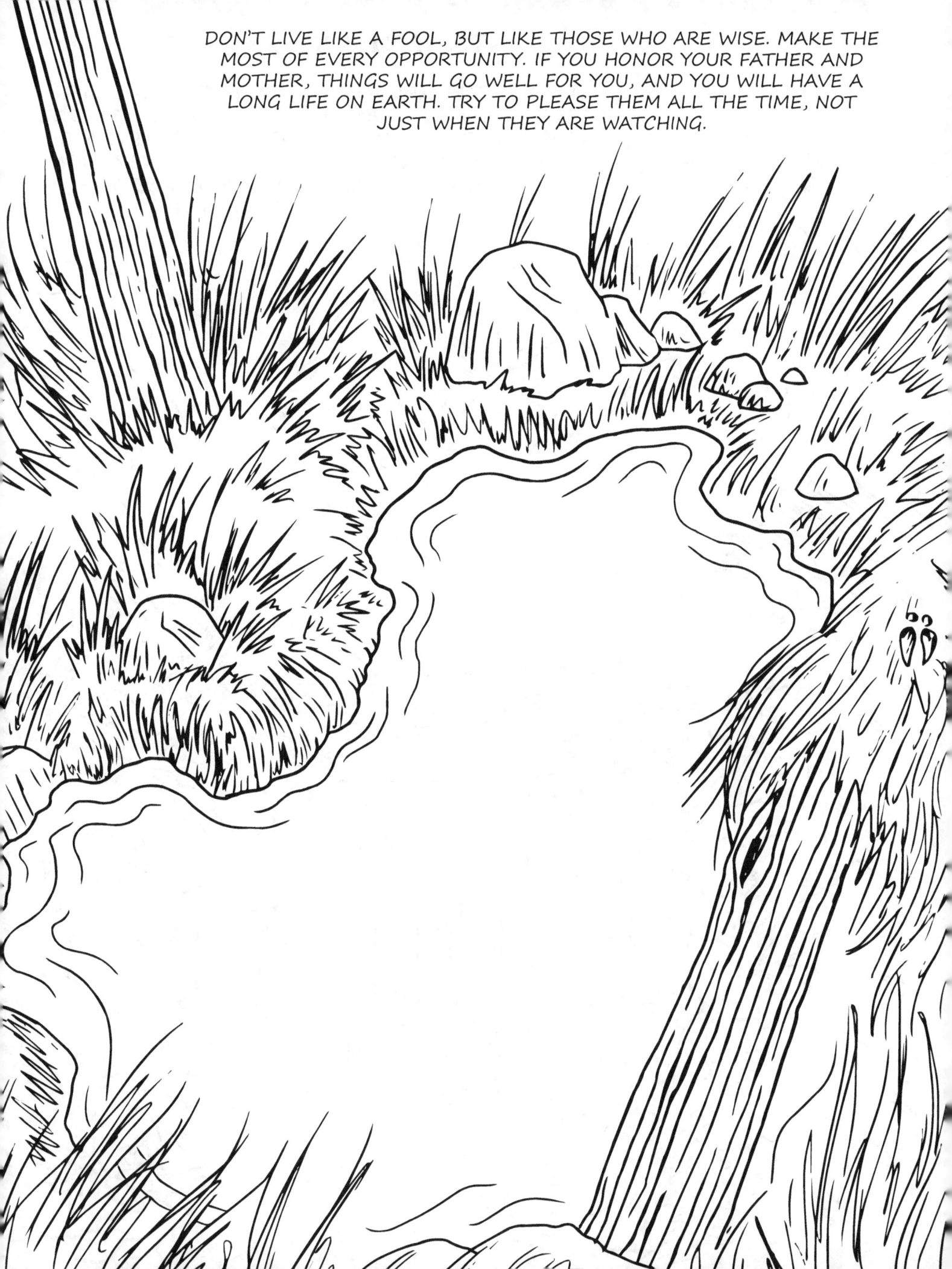

STEWARDS OF THE LAND

A GOOD STEWARD UNDERSTANDS THAT THE GIFT
PASSED DOWN TO THEM FOR SAFEKEEPING NEEDS TO
BE MANAGED AND MAINTAINED SO THAT IT CAN BE
PASSED DOWN FROM GENERATION TO GENERATION.
THE GRATITUDE I NEED TO RECEIVE AND THE
COMPASSION I NEED TO GIVE.

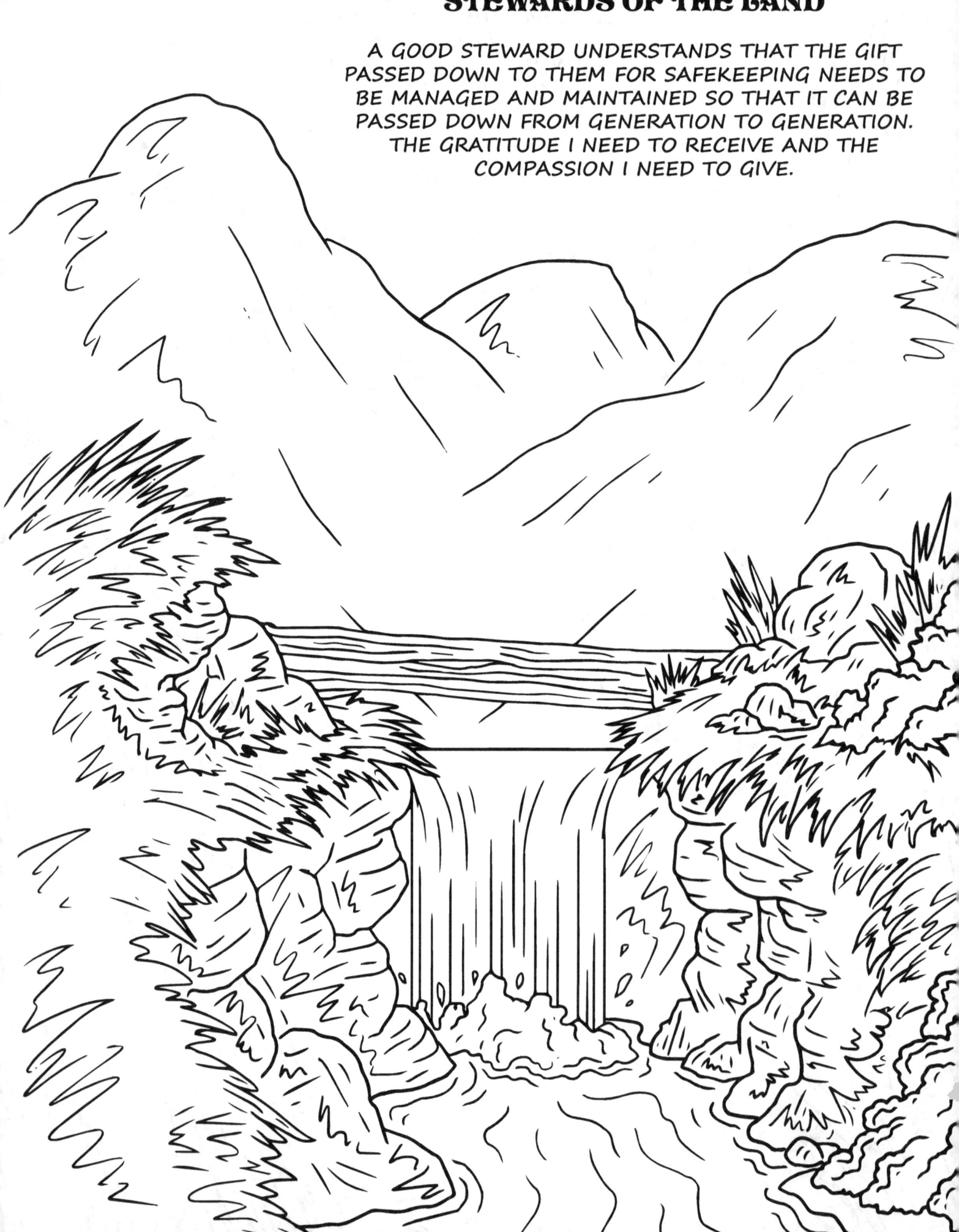

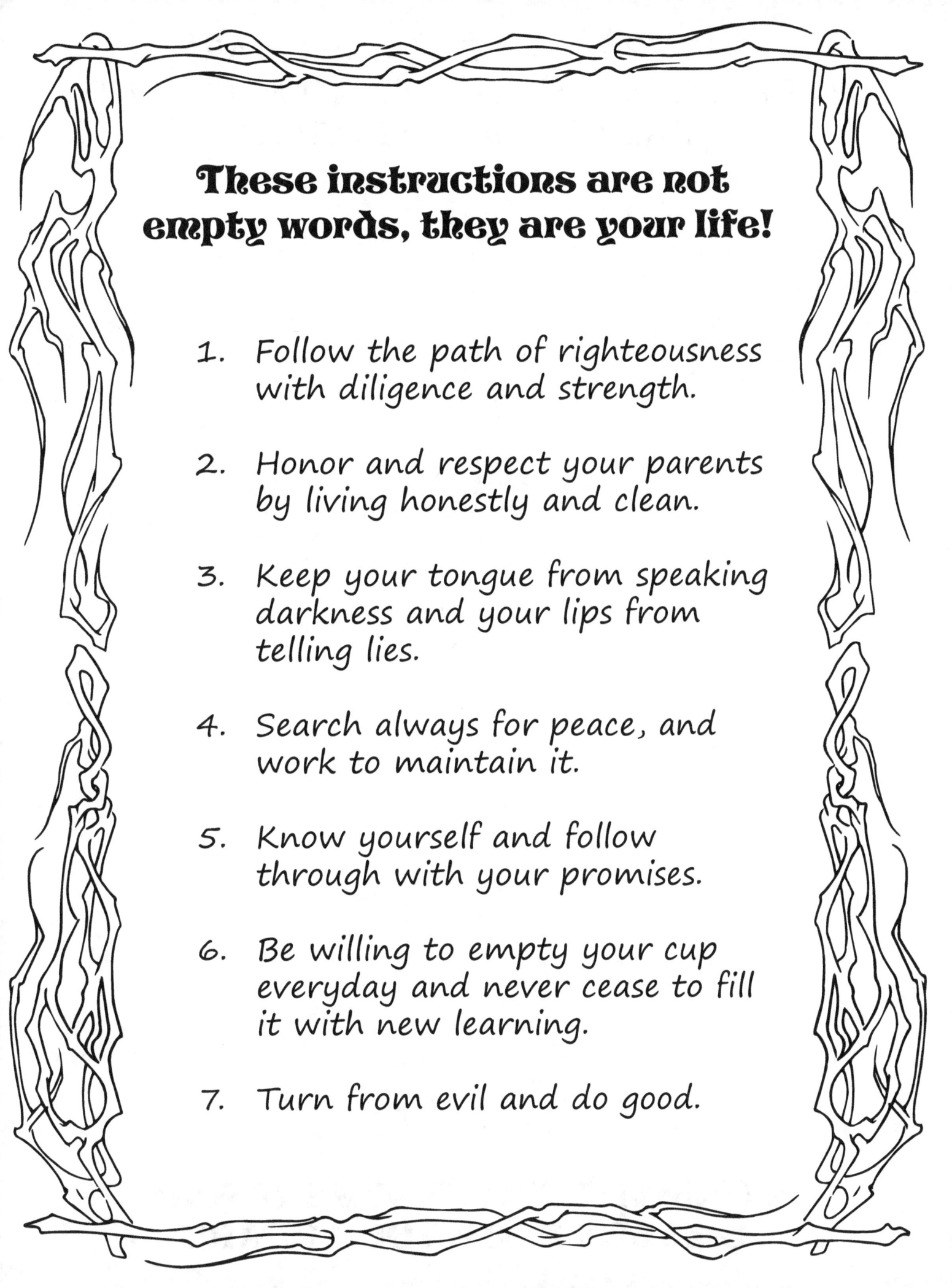

These instructions are not empty words, they are your life!

1. Follow the path of righteousness with diligence and strength.

2. Honor and respect your parents by living honestly and clean.

3. Keep your tongue from speaking darkness and your lips from telling lies.

4. Search always for peace, and work to maintain it.

5. Know yourself and follow through with your promises.

6. Be willing to empty your cup everyday and never cease to fill it with new learning.

7. Turn from evil and do good.

THE SPIRIT AND THE WILL ARE
PARTNERS IN THE BODY AND MUST FIND
BALANCE IN THE HEART.

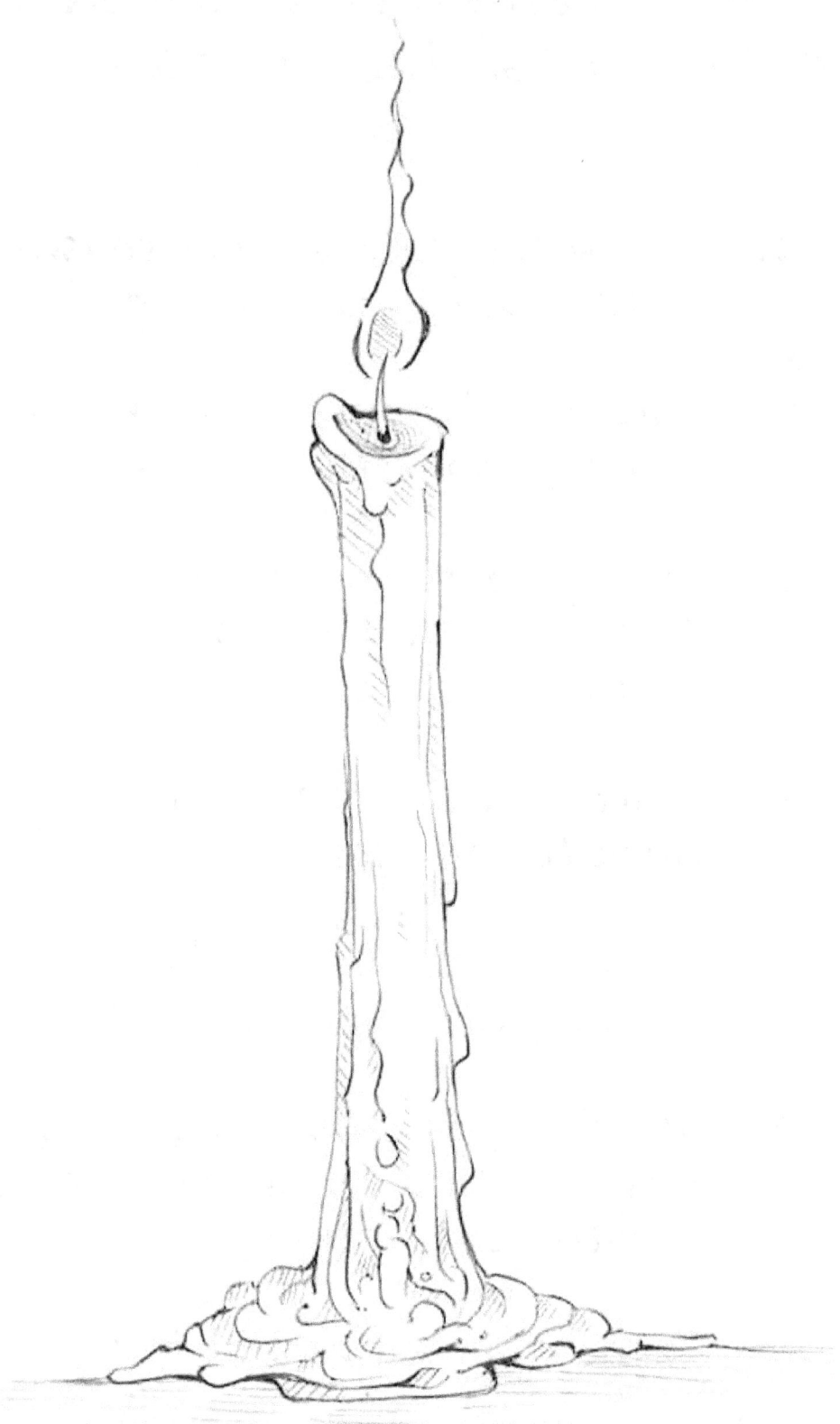

FORGIVE YOUR BROTHERS AND
SISTERS FROM YOUR HEART

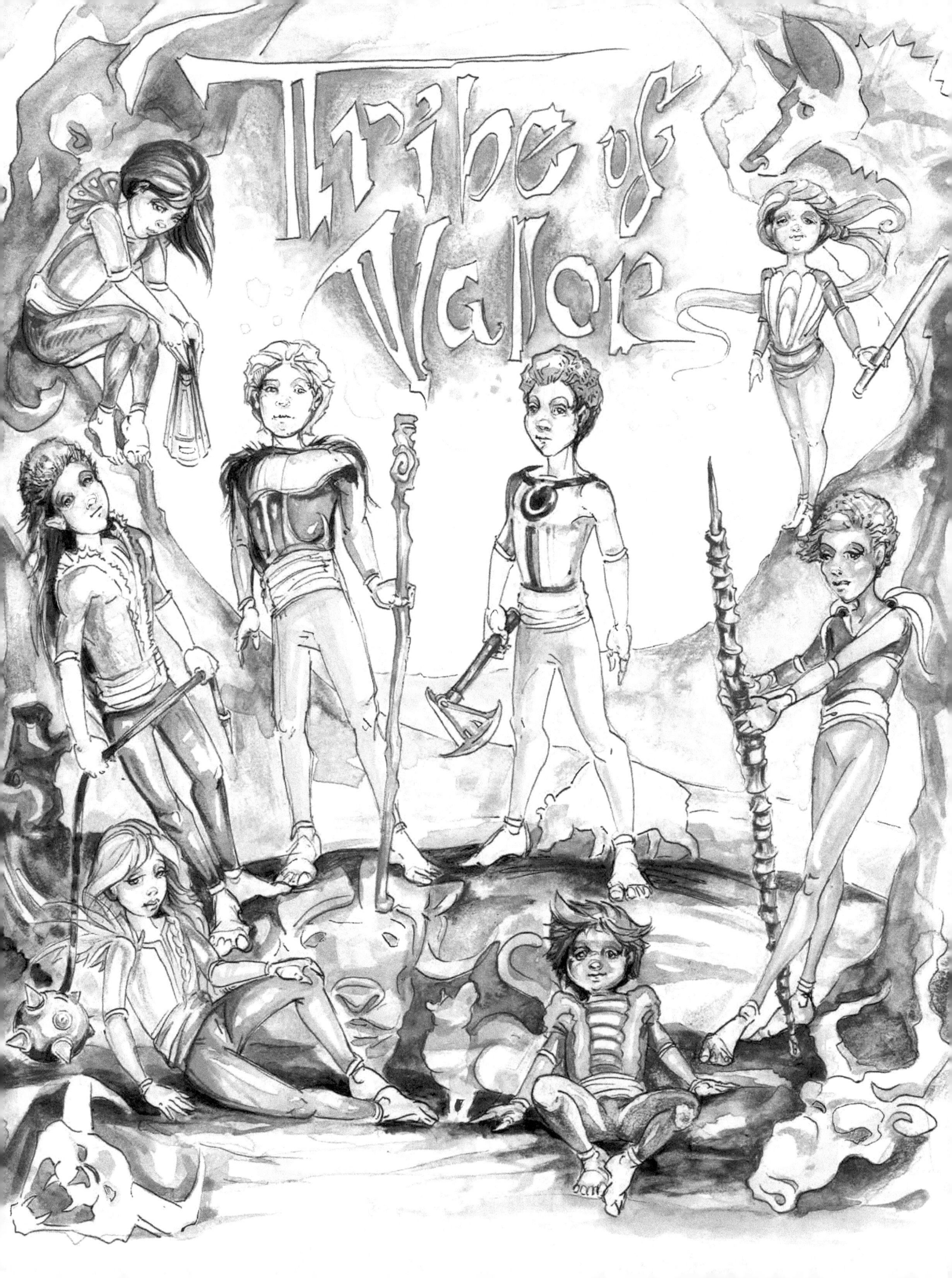

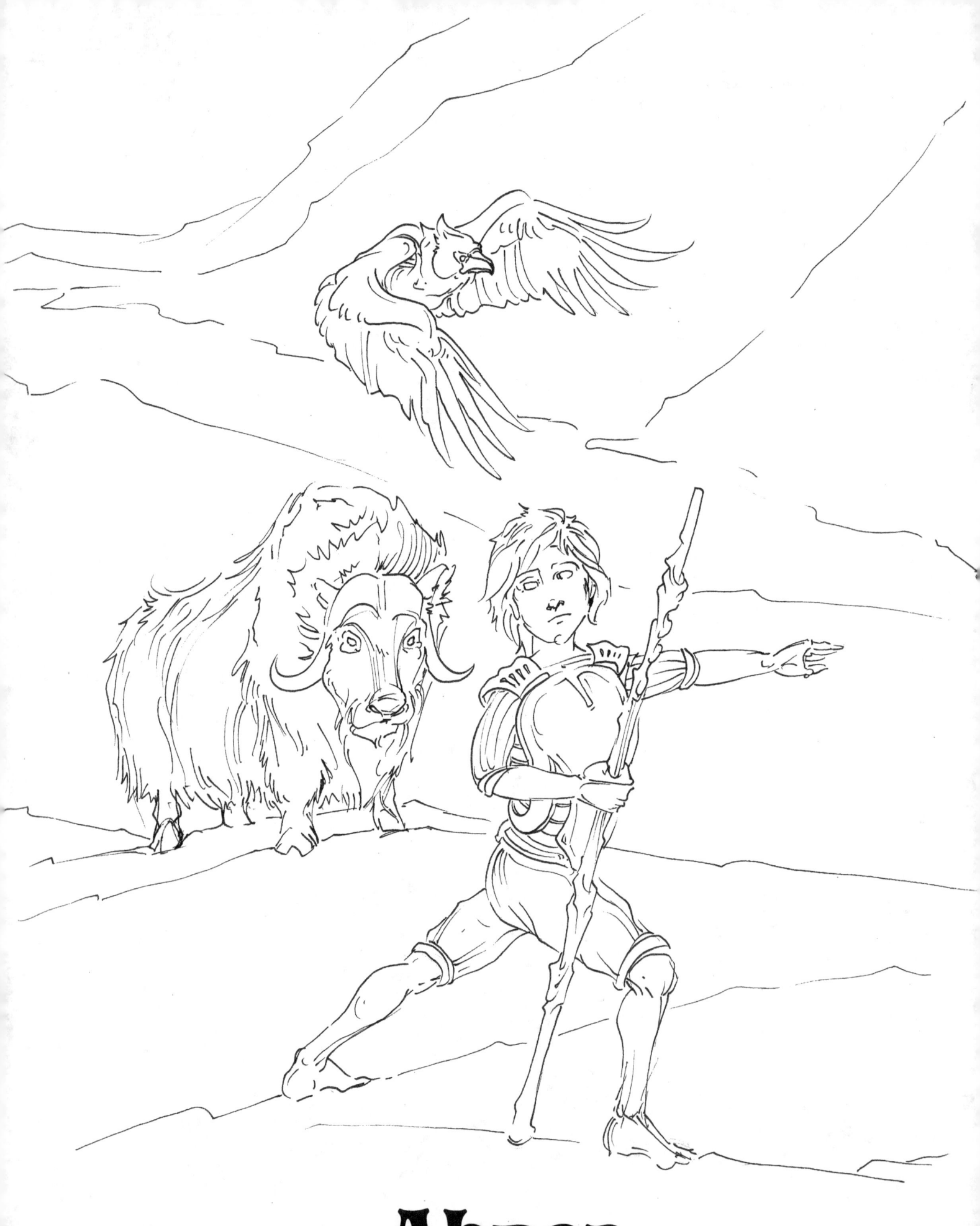

Abner

JOURNAL YOUR MEDITATION THOUGHTS...

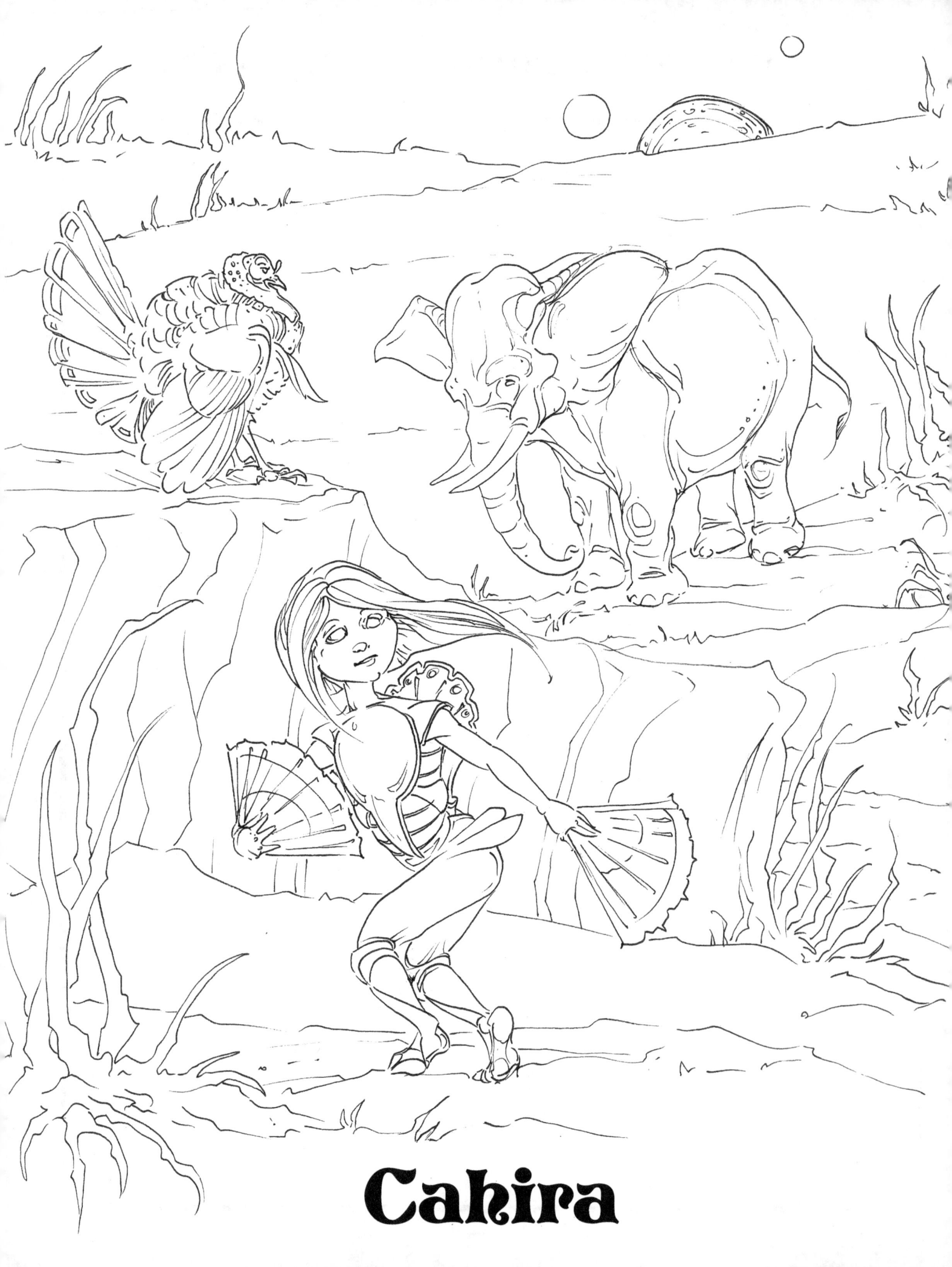

Cahira

JOURNAL YOUR MEDITATION THOUGHTS...

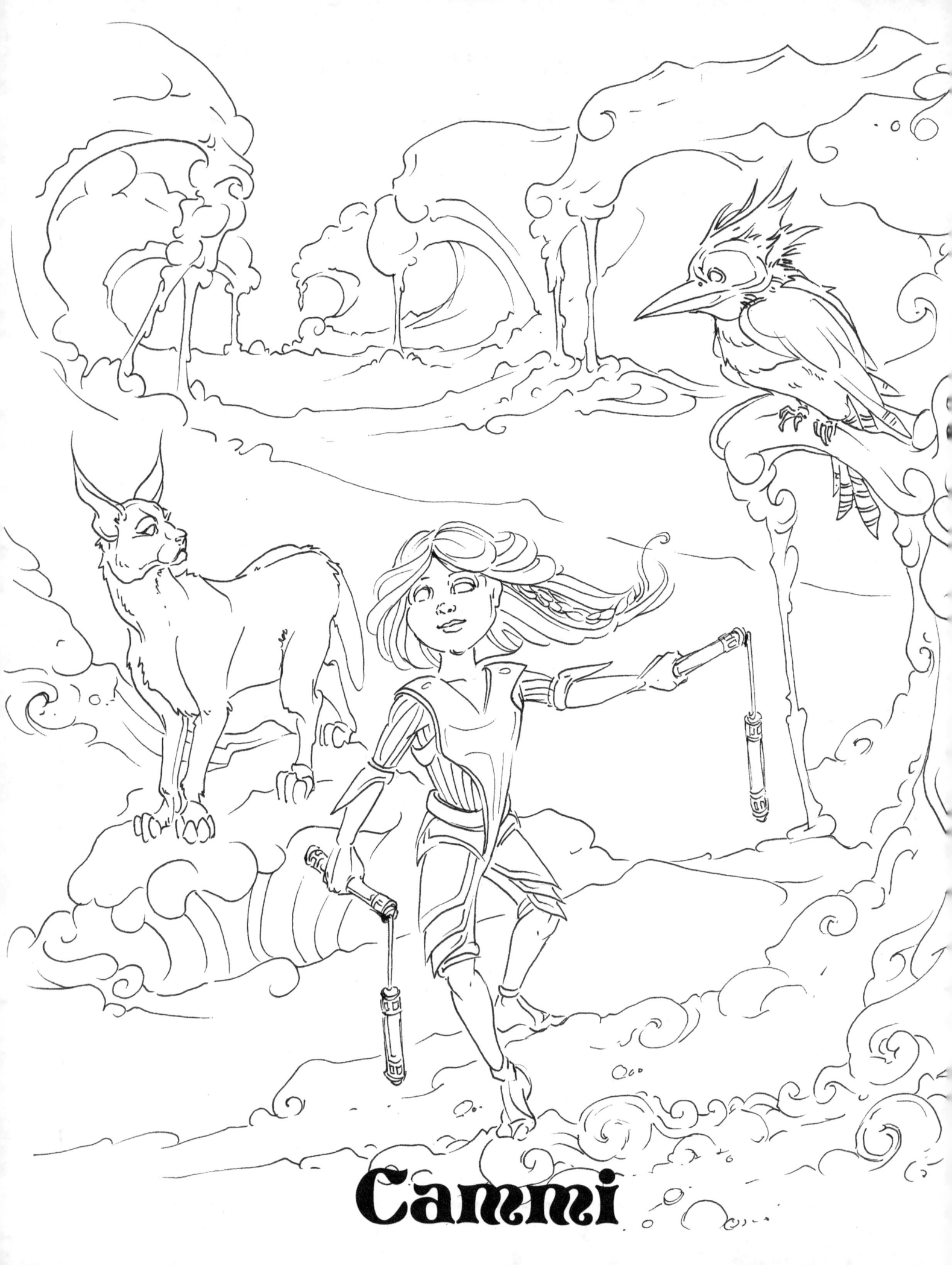

Cammi

JOURNAL YOUR MEDITATION THOUGHTS...

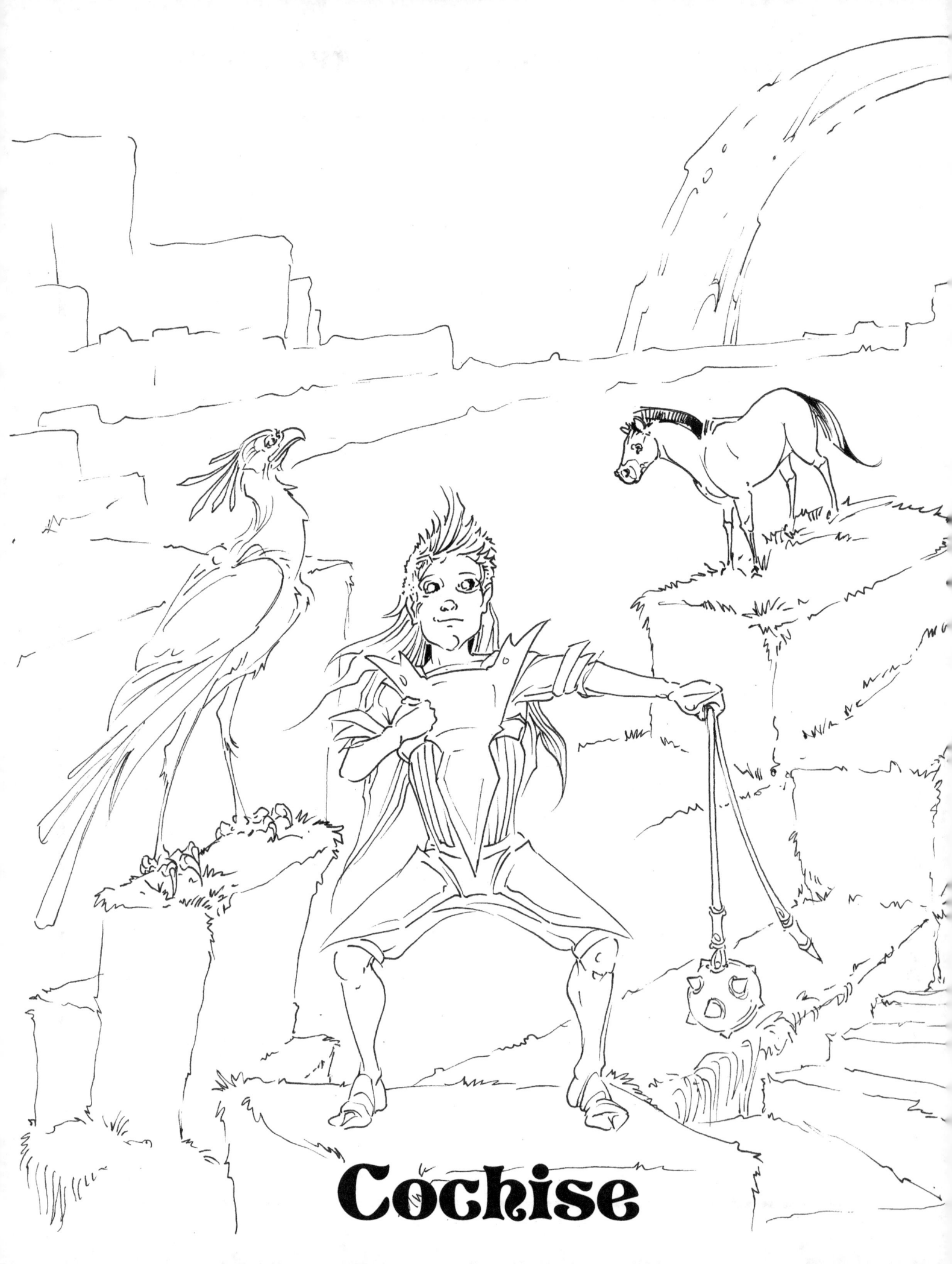

Cochise

JOURNAL YOUR MEDITATION THOUGHTS...

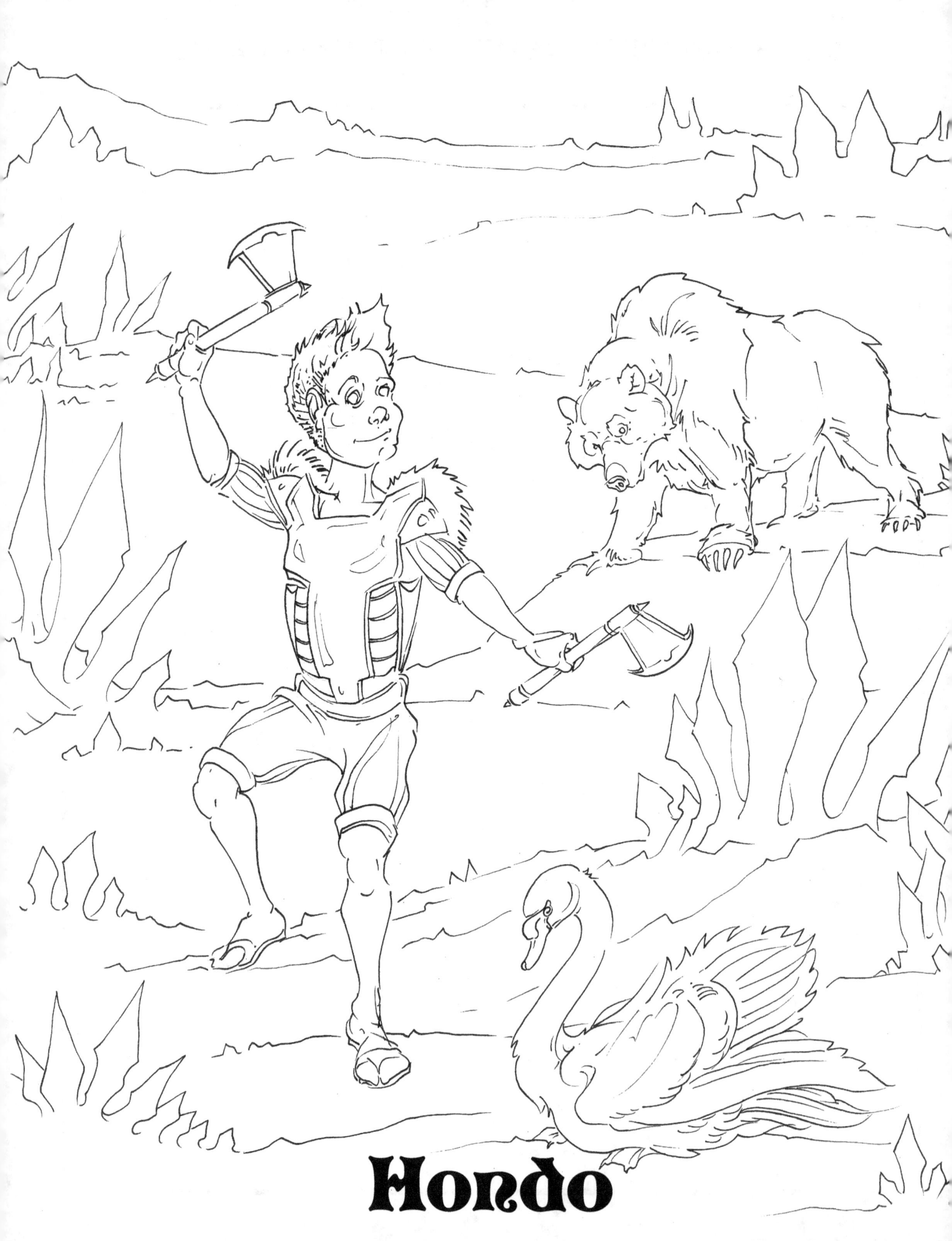

Hondo

JOURNAL YOUR MEDITATION THOUGHTS...

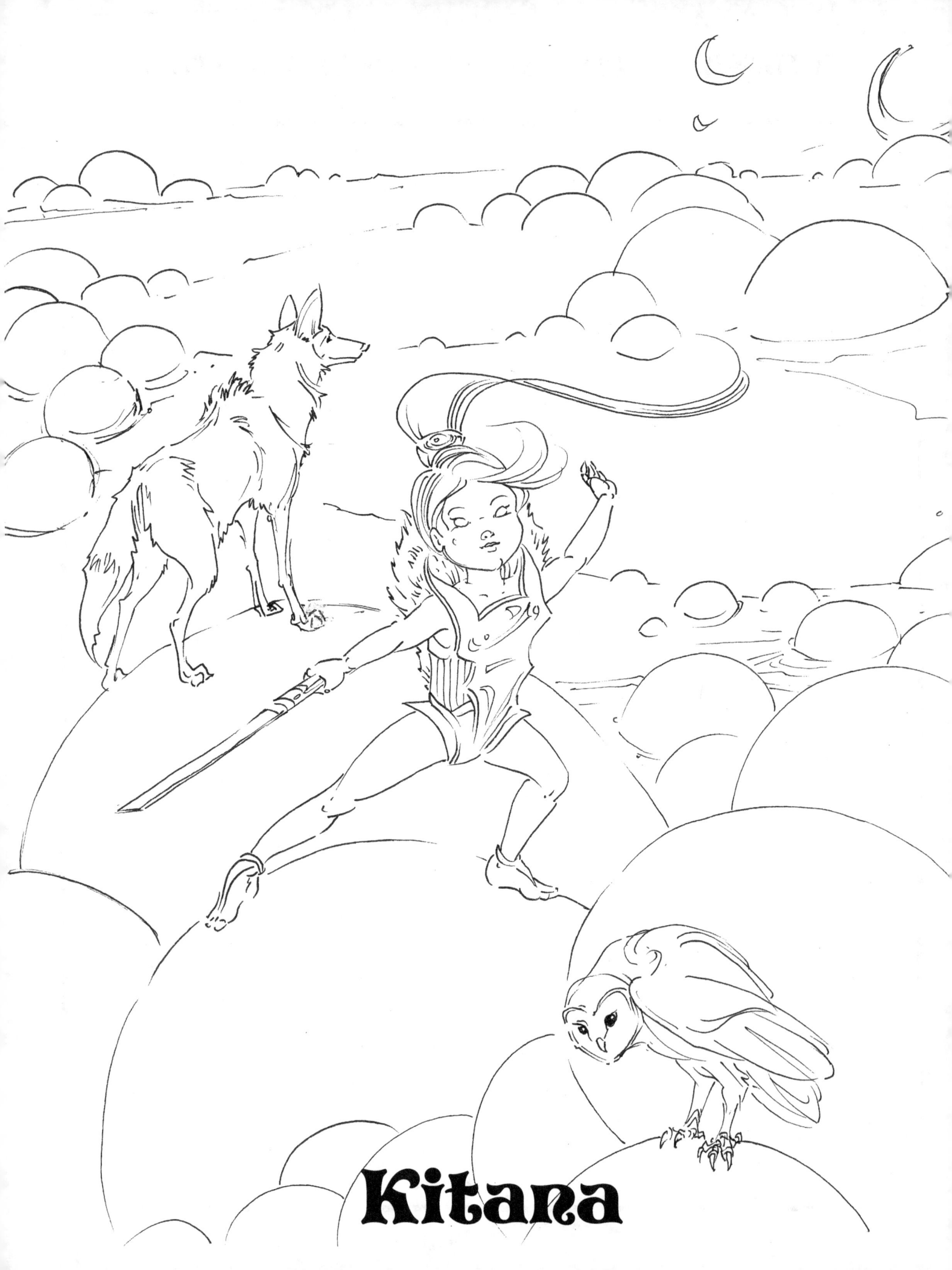

Kitana

JOURNAL YOUR MEDITATION THOUGHTS...

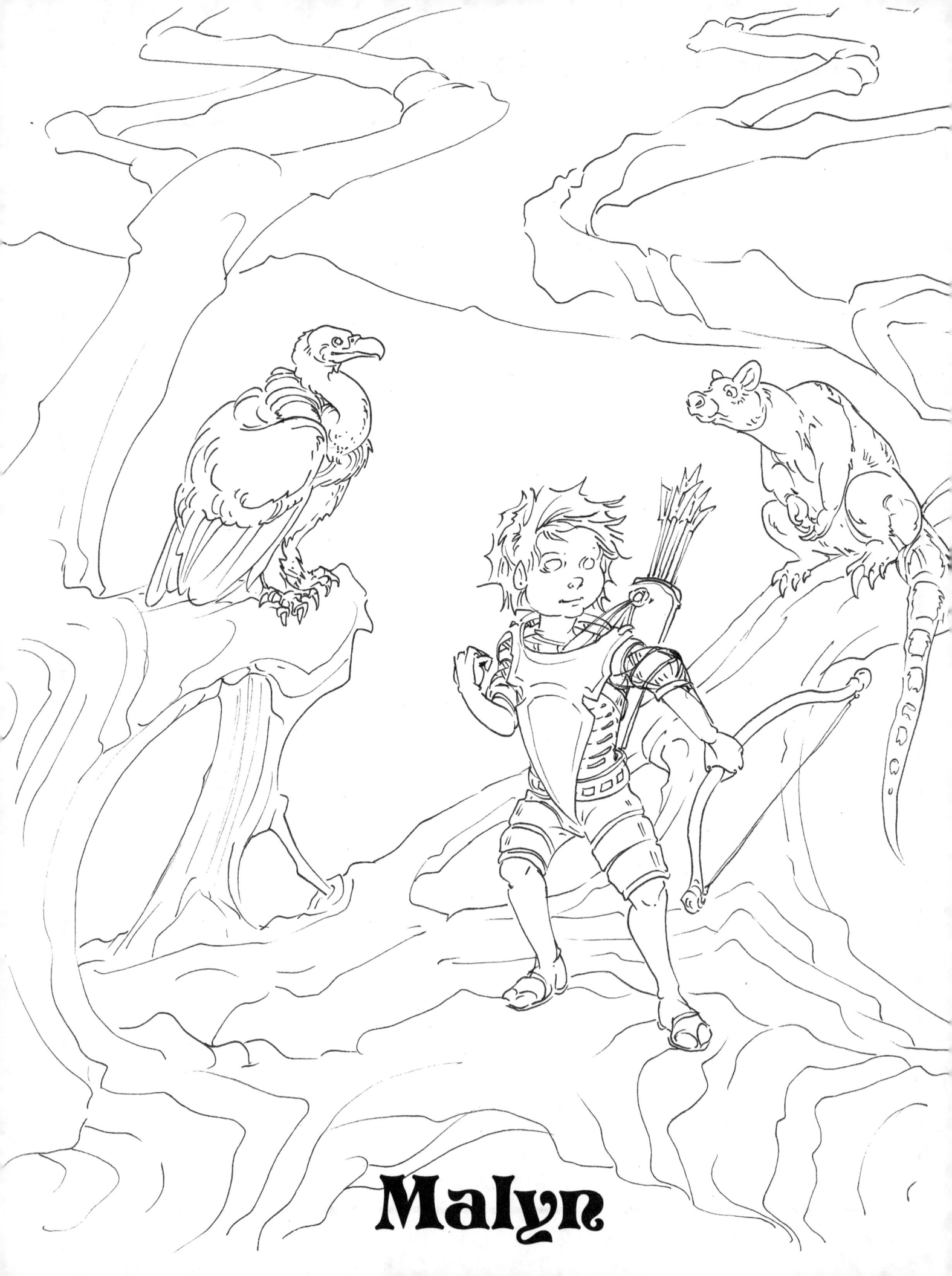

Malyn

JOURNAL YOUR MEDITATION THOUGHTS...

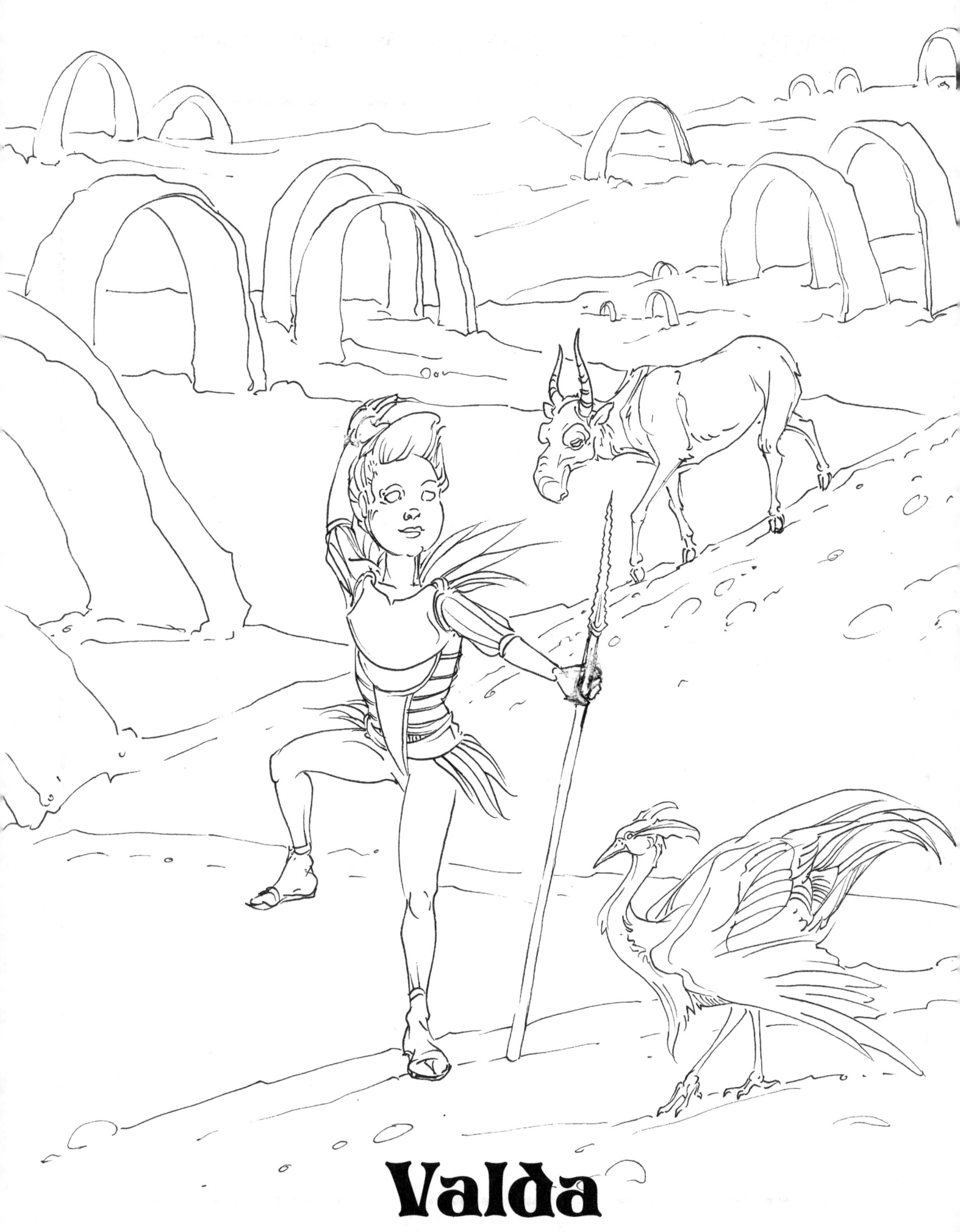

Valda

JOURNAL YOUR MEDITATION THOUGHTS...

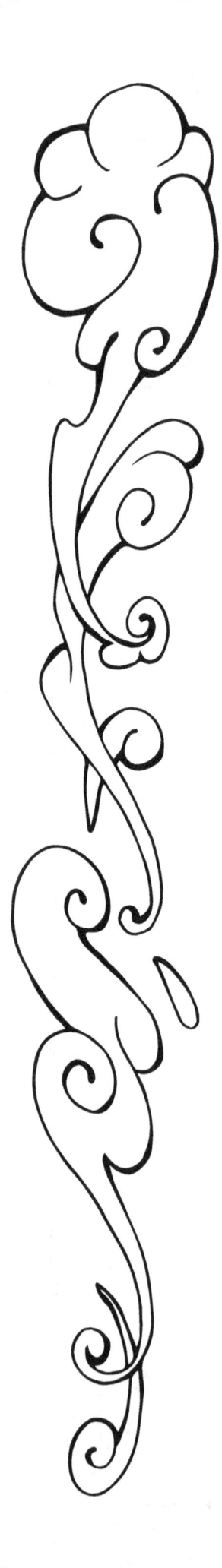
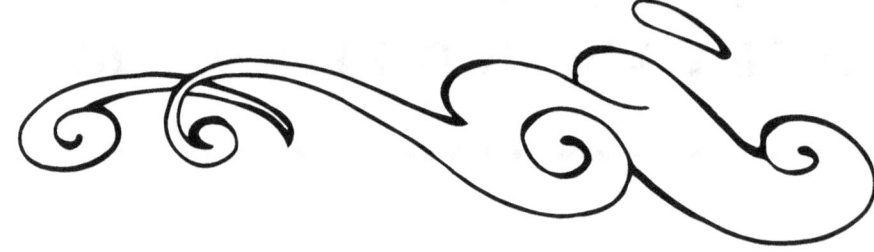

The sword and pen are mighty.

The signature of your
portrait is signed
with a pen.

Your art of living is
defended by a sword.

Practice both, until it
is the part that makes
you whole.

**On the following pages,
practice the art of the pen
by copying the phrases.**

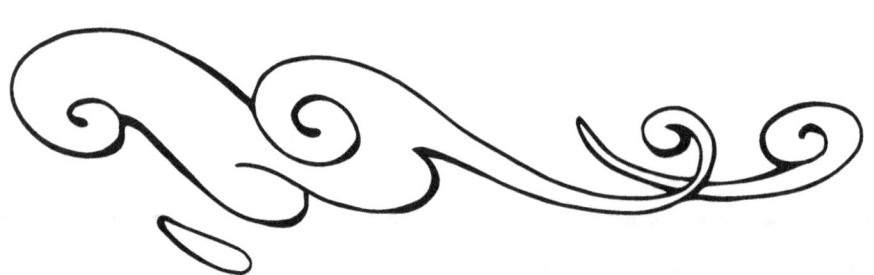

Be the river that perseveres through the mountains.

Respect is a universal language, speak it well.

Refuse to let the world corrupt you.

Deep roots make you want for nothing.

Patiently and constantly prefect your art.

Hold on to that which is good.

Good discipline makes anything you attempt possible.

Live peacefully with those around you.

If you are wise and understand, prove it by living honorably. The gateway to an honorable life is very narrow and the road is difficult. Only a few ever find it.

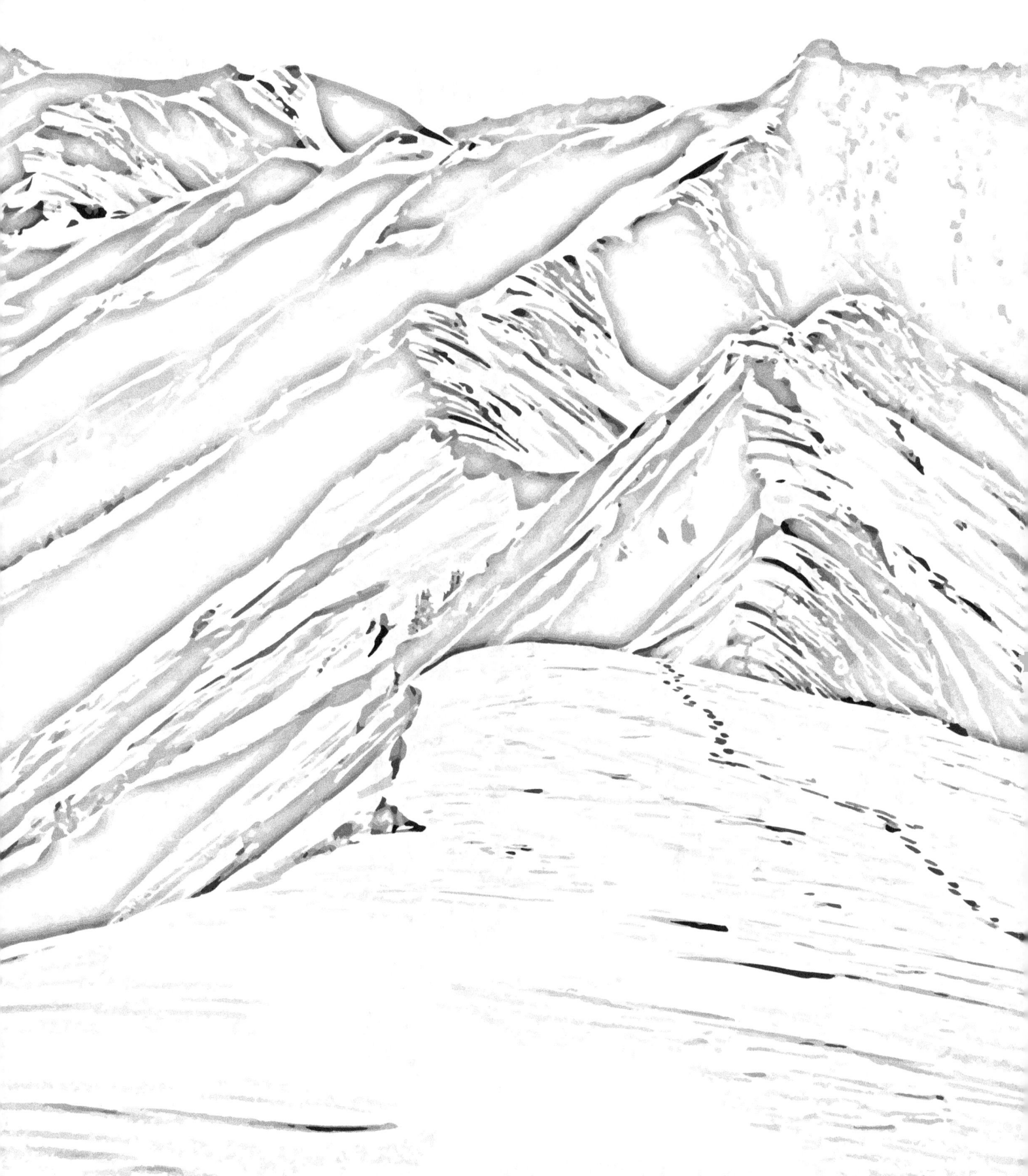

THE CREATORS

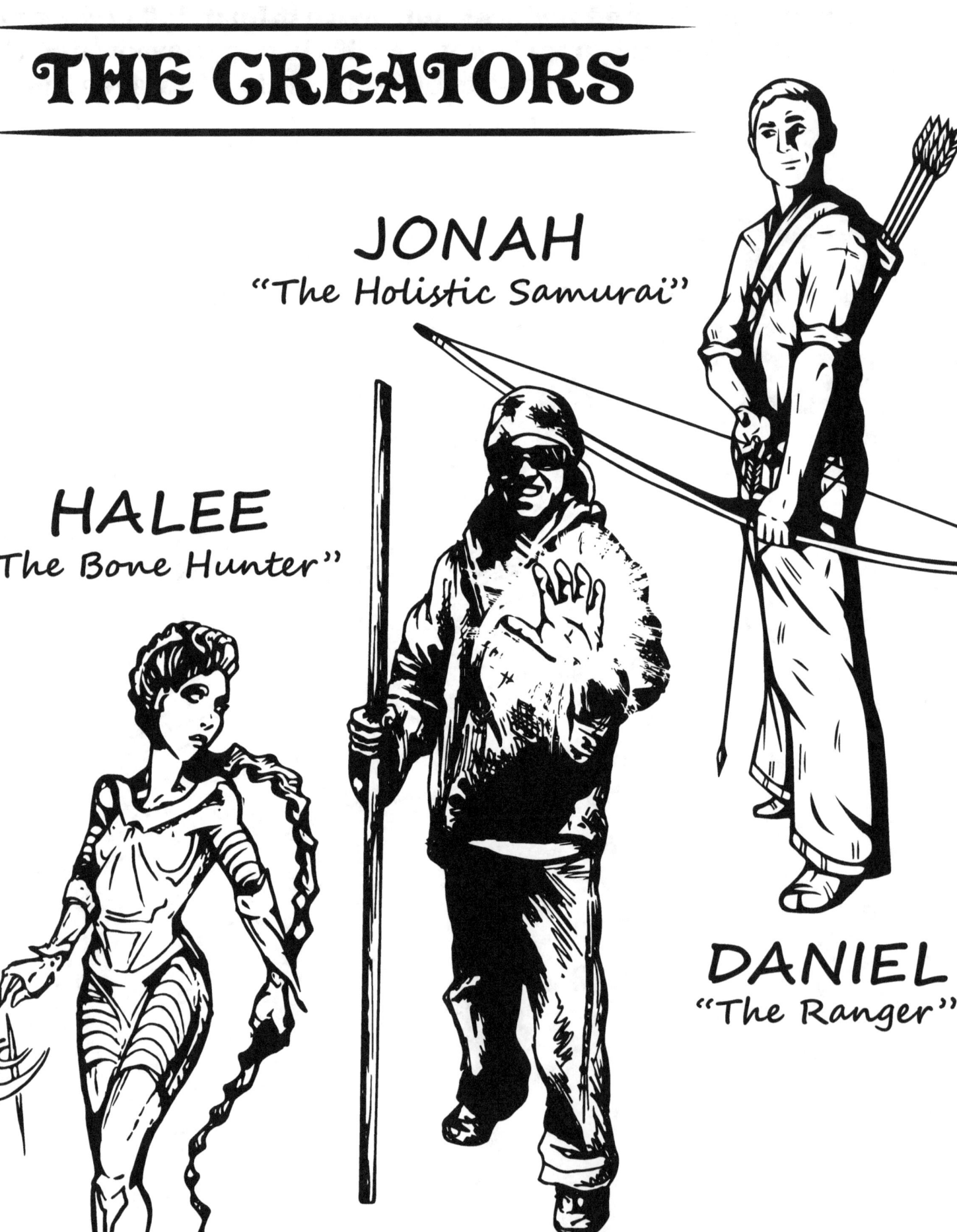

JONAH
"The Holistic Samurai"

HALEE
"The Bone Hunter"

DANIEL
"The Ranger"

www.ingramcontent.com/pod-product-compliance
Lightning Source LLC
Chambersburg PA
CBHW080841170526
45158CB00009B/2602